William Lord Watts

Snioland

Or, Iceland, its jokulls and fjalls

William Lord Watts

Snioland
Or, Iceland, its jokulls and fjalls

ISBN/EAN: 9783337318994

Printed in Europe, USA, Canada, Australia, Japan

Cover: Foto ©Andreas Hilbeck / pixelio.de

More available books at **www.hansebooks.com**

STRÖKER (*Frontispiece*).

SNIOLAND;

OR,

ICELAND,

Its Jokulls and Fjalls.

BY

WILLIAM LORD WATTS.

London:
LONGMANS AND CO., PATERNOSTER ROW.
1875.

LONDON:
PRINTED BY GILBERT AND RIVINGTON,
ST. JOHN'S SQUARE, AND WHITEFRIARS STREET, E.C.

TO

My Mother

I DEDICATE THIS BOOK,

AS AN ACKNOWLEDGMENT OF THE

INTEREST SHE HAS TAKEN IN MY TRAVELS,

AND THE

ASSISTANCE SHE HAS AFFORDED ME

IN THE

PREPARATION OF THIS WORK

FOR PUBLICATION.

PREFACE.

I have three objects in publishing the few following pages :—

First—It is my wish to direct the attention of the travelling public to a land (but little beyond the beaten track of tourists, and within the limit of a six weeks' holiday) that abounds in natural phenomena of equal interest to the geologist and the physical geographer.

Secondly—To inform habitual travellers, many of whom have already visited Iceland, that in that island are tracts of land and mountain solitudes which have never been explored; and to remind them that amongst these untrodden fastnesses have occurred some of the mightiest phenomena the world has ever witnessed, of which we know nothing certain, either of their birthplace or their character, and scarcely anything of their effects.

Thirdly—To take this opportunity of expressing my most earnest wish for more co-operation among travellers generally. I have no doubt there are many men who have the *ability* and the *inclination* to undertake the work of exploration I propose, and who yet feel that individually they have not sufficient means to carry out such an undertaking; for the "sinews of war" are likewise the sinews of travel. If men of this class and disposition were to co-operate, much might be accomplished, and these lands of mystery be made known.

If I could meet with three men, who knew what they were going to undertake when they decided on attempting to make the exploration of Iceland, who felt themselves equal to the task, and who would share the expense and co-operate loyally with me, I have no doubt that in three months we might throw great light upon these unknown tracts and mountains.

To those who wish for a simple vacation tour, a visit to Iceland recommends itself in many ways. The voyage is short and the climate is very healthy; the visitor will enjoy a total change, utterly different from the frequented track of continental travel, and will find in it an abundance of objects of fresh interest and research, which will well repay the efforts he may have made to reach them.

To men who have more leisure and means at their disposal, I would explain that the object of my next visit to Iceland will be the further investigation of Vatna Jökull, and the volcano upon the northern side of it, whose frequent eruptions have alone proclaimed its existence; and the exploration of the Odatherhaun, with its surrounding mountains. If time allows, I hope to include an examination of the land between Vatna and Langs Jökull, together with Langs and Hofs Jökulls.

The Appendix of this little work affords information as to the cost and plan of operation. I merely add that if there are three men who may read this, and feel they have the power and the wish to join me, I shall be happy to make their acquaintance through the Secretary of the Alpine Club.

In conclusion, I remark that this small volume does not pretend to be a treatise upon Iceland, but a simple narrative of the travels of the Rev. J. W—— and myself last year in that country, and as such is a "genuine record of genuine facts."

I will take this opportunity of thanking the Rev. Martin Hart for his kindness in allowing me to use the photographs Nos. 3, 6 and 12, which were taken by him.

W. L. WATTS.

LIST OF ILLUSTRATIONS.

                                                             FACING PAGE

No. 1. Ströker, *Frontispiece*.

No. 2. Almanna Gjá 14

No. 3. View of Almanna Gjá, with Measure Stone, from door of Church at Thingvellir 40

No. 4. View of Logsberg from the back of farm at Thingvellir, with Arnann's Fell in the distance . . 52

No. 5. Great Geyser in eruption 66

No. 6. Basin of Geyser when empty 78

No. 7. Encampment at Geyser (taken in 1871) . . . 92

No. 8. Hills behind Geyser 104

No. 9. View of River Oxera 118

No. 10. Waterfall at Thingvellir 130

No. 11. Church and Farmhouse at Thingvellir . . 144

No. 12. View of a Solfatara at Krisuvick . . 156

SNIOLAND;

OR,

ICELAND, ITS JÖKULLS AND FJALLS.

———◆———

AFTER lounging about for a week at Edinburgh, in June, 1874, we took our places on board the "Diana," in company with a lively party of Danes, who had, no doubt, been looking forward to the invasion of us Britishers. Having seen our twenty boxes, with numerous other packages, portmanteaus, &c., carefully stowed away, I tried to find how many of the old faces I had become acquainted with in my former voyage of 1871 still remained. Among the passengers I was agreeably surprised to find Mr. Tompson, a Danish merchant of Reykjavick. Upon leaving the Frith of Forth, the volcanic formation of the mountains in this part of Scotland is very apparent, especially when sailing in a NE. direction. The "saddle-backed" volcano, Arthur's Seat, first comes prominently to view. There can be no doubt as to the force which created the surrounding mountains; a survey of the continuous line of elevations, almost from the above-named mountain to the little conical hill upon the main land, opposite the Bass Rock, as well as the Bass Rock itself, confirms the opinion that they are of volcanic origin; and the comparison of these mountains with those of the Faroe Isles and Iceland attests the truth of such a conclusion.

Upon rising next morning the appearance of the sky was anything but satisfactory; the sunrise was brilliant, though the sky was "greasy," and screwy pieces of cloud were dispersed throughout the heavens. The barometer, however, was high, and the wind NNW. Towards midday it blew half a gale, a heavy sea rose, and we were almost all seasick except the Danes, who with few exceptions, I have often remarked, seldom suffer from that malady.

June 4th.—Wind and sea were unabated; the wind had shifted to the east, and it was raining. The barometer fell half an inch. I felt unusually pugnacious with Dibdin and other writers who have advocated and sung the delights of " life on the ocean wave, and a home on the rolling deep," &c. In fact, the very attribute of *rolling*, which seems to have delighted the poet, is the very thing I object to. The "Diana" is a gunboat which seems built with every facility for rolling, and after a short voyage in her, one feels very much as if one had been living in an American churn.

About 7 P.M. we reached Thorshaven, but it was impossible to land, owing to the tempest that was blowing. Two boats came off through the surf, and with excellent skill managed to hang on to leeward of us. A pilot came on board from the first boat, but as it was not possible to land or take in coal, we made for Kings' Haven, which is a much better harbour than that of Thorshaven. We were astonished to see how near the pilot and captain deemed it safe to approach the lee shore. Here, as around the Scottish isles, there is deep water quite close to the land; the depth at this part, a mile from the shore, is 100 fathoms, while we anchored only 100 yards from land in twelve fathoms of water. I could not learn there had ever been any variation in the depth of any of these fjords, therefore the volcanic forces, among these islands at any rate, seem to be "played out." This depth of water so close to land is, I believe, peculiar to many volcanic islands.

The Faroe Islands, which are about twenty in number, are entirely of volcanic formation, usually rising in terraces of basalt directly from the sea. The rocks abound in mineral specimens, principally of the zeolitic family; the "noble" and "fire" opal are also found here, though they are by no means common. I tried to buy some specimens, but none appeared to have been found very recently; one of the Feroese merchants remarked that "he did not think it had been a good year for them," a way of putting it which seemed to imply that he considered them a species of vegetable, whose growth depended upon the nature of the season.

June 5th.—Still at anchor, with the wind blowing NNE., and a heavy leaden sky, through which the sun was struggling. The barometer had slightly risen. I had a long talk with our pilot, who informed me that the Feroe Eya (Feroe Islands) meant Sheep Islands; that they possessed a very equable climate, and that contrary to our experience in England, the month of May in this year had been a very fine month; that he could see no difference in the climate now and fifty years ago, and he considered the Islands were equally healthy during each season of the year. Indeed the climate must be the quintessence of all that is wholesome and invigorating, or the diseases arising from the worst possible sanitary arrangements would soon depopulate the Islands.

We were now lying in a sheltered fjord, the NE. banks of which rose in a series of basaltic terraces, capped to the NE. and NW. with hills where patches of snow were still lying in clefts and sheltered places. The largest mountain rises to a peak, cleft in the centre, as my companion W—— said, like Scuir-na-Gelean, in the Island of Skye. Many of the passengers amused themselves with fishing over the stern of the vessel. Several small plaice and a large cod were caught; in and on the latter we found a number of parasitic insects.

After lunch the captain made several soundings, and when the anchor was weighed, it brought up a lump of calcareous matter, principally composed of broken and partly-decomposed shells, black sand, and mud. The weather had now considerably moderated, and we steered for Thorshaven. Upon leaving our shelter, we were surprised to see in how sinuous a harbour we had taken refuge: at its mouth we noticed the peculiar band of ruffled water, almost amounting to a bore, which is perceptible in places where the wind or tide meets any of the strong currents which occur in the waters around many of these islands; these currents are sometimes so strong as to require eight men to pull a boat against them.

We were soon anchored in the Bay of Thorshaven, and we amused ourselves till midnight fishing over the ship's side. It was quite light throughout the night; in these northern latitudes one is continually deceived as to time.

June 6*th*.—I started with C—— early in the morning to cross the Island to the ruined Church of Kirkuboer upon the north side. After reaching the shore in a coaling boat, we passed through the town, and proceeded up a glen to the west, which nearly crosses the Island. It came on to rain heavily, and by the time we reached the ridge of hills which terminates the glen and divides it from the sea upon the west, we were nearly wet through. After ascending to the height of 600 feet, we crossed the mountain ridge, and descended to the sea, a mile and a half from the ruins of Kirkuboer. Our way then lay along the beach, over an immense accumulation of kelp and other sea-weed, and we picked up a piece of sponge attached to a fragment of mussel-shell, a somewhat remarkable occurrence in these latitudes. We reached the church, and after inspecting the ruins, which are of the twelfth century, at the request of the farmer, whose farm adjoins, we took some refreshment at his house. He was a fine specimen of a Feroese, being tall and well built. He welcomed us most cordially, and though he spoke no English, we managed to make him understand how much we appreciated his kindness. He ushered us into a cheerful little room looking out upon the narrow channel which divides the Island Stromoe from Kotta, and Hestoe from the neighbouring islands; and pro-

ALMANNA GJÁ.

vided us with an ample repast of butter, " Twœ Bakka,"[1] coffee and cigars. We showed him our telescope, aneroid, and compass, which seemed greatly to interest him, and we departed speculating as to whether he was descended from the builders of the church, the ruins of which we had been admiring. We visited the little church opposite, where at my last visit in 1871 I had seen some beautiful carving; it was now undergoing repair, and the carving and a quaint old painting of the Lord's Supper, which had previously stood over the altar, were removed. I inquired about them, and the Feroese who were repairing the church at once set off to an outhouse to bring the carving and painting for our inspection. We could only determine who three of the figures were intended to represent, viz., Christ, St. John, and Judas with the bag. We pointed out that the painter had made but eleven apostles; one of the men ingeniously attempted to explain matters by saying it was quite right, counting our Lord in to make the twelfth.

The weather having cleared, we examined the basaltic cliffs behind the farm, collecting several fragments containing zeolites, principally natrolite and chabasite. There was a magnificent view of the surrounding hills, which here assume a variety of fantastic forms. Returning, we took a survey of the town of Thorshaven. Irregular and narrow streets of wooden houses, roofed with turf, are clustered together upon the hill-side in the NW. corner of the bay, built in defiance of every sanitary and architectural law; that the inhabitants are not decimated by fever must be an additional proof as to the great salubrity of the climate.

We set sail about 6 P.M., passing through the beautiful islands to the west and north of Thorshaven. Sickness prevented me from noticing anything more, except a specimen of chrysocollite, shown me by a French gentleman; this mineral abounds in some parts of these islands.

June 7th was therefore a blank. The next day repaid us for all our inconveniences: we woke to a beautiful view of Berufjörde, with the snow-capped hills around it, and the vessel lay in calm water. Before us were weird black mountains and conical hills, whose rugged outlines peering through the snow spoke plainly of ancient volcanic activity, and of the grim agency which gave them birth. The season appeared late, for the snow was lying abundantly low down upon the sides of the mountains, and the cold wind which blew from the distant "Jökulls" froze the water that had been used to swab the decks. Depositing the mail and a lady passenger, we steamed out of the fjord and along the coast towards Reykjavick. The coast-line as seen from the sea appears a continuous chain of volcanic mountains, heavily capped with snow, from which glaciers sweep down to the plain beneath; but the land intervening between the sea and the mountains is unobservable at the distance from which we viewed it. Having recovered from the *mal de mer*, I inquired whether there had been any variation in soundings along the coast, or in the coast-line; I could not learn that there had been any alteration of either in the history of the navigation of this part. There is a tradition in one of the sagas concerning vessels entering various fjords and sailing where it would be now impossible to take anything larger than a fishing-boat; but the ancient skjald's ideas of a vessel and ours no doubt materially differ. Mr. Tompson told me that a tract of land which used to be fields near Erribakki is now covered with water, but this may result from some variation in the flow of the river Hvità, and not from any volcanic disturbance or encroachment of the sea. Several gentlemen on board who had witnessed the eruption of the unknown volcano in Vatna Jökull in 1873, while they were staying at Erribakki, described the smoke and reflection as being directly in a line with Hecla, and the appearance was such that when first observed the eruption was supposed to be from that mountain.

June 9th.—A gale compelled us to lie to, for we could not steam against the heavy wind.

June 10th.—We reached the Westerman Isles: they are even more grotesque in appearance than the Faroe, and their decidedly volcanic nature is still more marked. Every ledge was crowded with sea fowl, the cry of which when heard in the distance resembles that of a pack of hounds in full chase. Here and upon the west coast of Iceland the big brown gull is found.

We left the mail, and steamed away, wondering how the inhabitants managed to spend their time upon such outlandish and desolate spots, for the "Diana" is often compelled to pass them by, in consequence of bad weather or fog. We had a fine view of Hecla, which was still covered with snow. About midday we lost sight of the Westermans, and rounded the Cape Reykjaness. Here we first saw lava streams. These had flowed down from several ancient volcanic vents, and formed, together with large masses of coloured tufa, a very weird and grand sight, and also one very peculiar in its character to Iceland.

By 8 P.M. we were entering the Bay of Reykjavick. The bright rays of the evening sun were illuminating the beautiful Mount Esjia still wrapped in its winter clothing, upon the NE. side of the Bay. A few fleecy evening clouds were collecting round its flattened summit, and creeping down its steep black sides, deepening the shadow on the side from which the sunlight had departed, and clinging like masses of wool to the sunlit summit, and the western face of the mountain. Far in the NW. horizon was the snowy pointed mass of Snæfells "Jökull." Upon the opposite side of the Bay lay the straggling capital of Iceland, Reykjavick, with its wooden houses and stores, which brought vividly to remembrance the "frame houses" which spring up with such mushroom-like growth in the frontier towns and upon the plains of NW. America; the main difference being that Reykjavick is as slow in its progression as America is rapid. The town was gay with flags, crowds clustered upon the wooden landing stages, and boat-loads of people were coming off to the ship. Several other craft were lying in the Bay, and as the "Diana" took up her place between a Danish and French man-of-war, which are stationed here to look after the fisheries; a band upon the Danish vessel saluted us with a few popular national strains of welcome.

After the usual salutations from officials and a few friends, we supped; fully appreciating the comfort of a vessel at anchor, instead of one rolling about as if trying every possible means of producing discomfort. It was broad daylight when we came out on deck; at 12 p.m. the sun had scarcely sunk beneath the horizon, the western sky reflected a grandly-coloured brilliance, glowing with carmine, which passing through various gradations of colour and splendour, finally melted away in a wide-spread flood of pale yellowish green light, which lost itself in the deep blue of the sub-Arctic firmament. A bright spot high in the east told of fine weather for the day which was dawning, and warned us to seek the necessary rest to refresh us for the duties of the morrow.

June 11*th*.—We landed at 10 a.m. and at once sought a place to pitch our tent, for one can always endure delay (which by the way is always an unpleasantly prominent feature of travel) better in camp than anywhere else. I suppose the reason why time passes the most easily when camping out is that full employment is found in doing so many things for oneself that would otherwise be done for one, and as we were under the necessity of waiting some time while a man was despatched into the country to purchase fifteen horses, we could not do better than avail ourselves of this agreeable mode of passing time. We decided on camping upon a piece of ground close to the sea shore, at the back of the town; it belonged to the governor, who kindly allowed us to pitch our tent there. After dining I took a turn round the town, and found but little alteration in it since 1871.

As usual the prevailing element was fish wherever one looked; there were fish of all sorts, and all sizes, in all stages of salting and drying. Stacks of fish were piled up high and dry upon the beach; thousands were lying out upon the rocks preparatory to being cured; men and horses were carrying fish about, and small armies of ponies were waiting patiently with great packages of fish on either side of them ready to convey this great necessary of life inland for home consumption. Ships were lying in the harbour to carry off their share to other parts of the world, and boats were constantly coming in with fresh supplies. What the date is to the Arab, or the beefsteak to the Englishman, stockfish is to the Icelander. It is the one thing necessary for his food; he eats it at all times; he prefers it to everything else, and his nation's flag unfurled displays a stockfish as the emblem of its strength.

In the morning we saw a whale spouting in the sea in front of our encampment, but although whales often frequent the harbour of Reykjavick, it is very seldom they are caught.

June 12*th.*—We brought the remainder of our

things on shore, and made arrangements to engage an Icelander, Guthminder, as our guide, whom we despatched into the country to procure horses for us.

Our encampment was evidently the talk of the town, for at Reykjavick, as well as in other small places, anything out of the ordinary way, is sure to be a nine days' wonder. In this remote little capital, where everything from time immemorial has gone on strictly according to old-fashioned routine, there is "a lion in the path" against every infringement of rule or novelty of proceeding. It was astonishing to hear the puerile objections made to any mode of action out of the usual course. For instance, when we spoke to a man about camping by the shore, he said we must not do so, as we should disturb the eider ducks. Now, as a number of men were engaged drying fish upon the beach exactly opposite to our proposed encampment, and people were constantly shooting along the shore, nothing could be more irrational, moreover the field was tenanted with cows, and I do not think there were any ducks there at all.

In the evening the son of the clergyman of Storruvellir—from whom I had received great kindness at my former sojourn on the island—paid us a visit. He was studying for the medical profession, and we had a long talk about the tapeworm, which is very prevalent in Iceland. He remarked that it was only when an animal secreted the embryo form of the tapeworm that tapeworm was the result, and that when an animal secreted the tapeworm it produced the embryo form.

June 13*th*.—The mail was made up, and for the first time I used the new Icelandic stamp; for in consequence of its emancipation Iceland now has a stamp of her own; up to this time Danish stamps only were in use. W—— visited Hafnarfjord and brought back several specimens of Hafnarfjordite.[2] As Reykjavick was no novelty to me, my time was chiefly spent in the tent, or walking amongst the great piles of fish, watching the landing of fishing boats. I had often noticed great rows and rings of fishes' heads upon the beach, looking all the more ghastly from being severed from the body, staring with their great vacant eyes, reminding one of the pagan rite which required a string of human heads as a propitiation. I had long wondered what they were intended for, and upon inquiring was informed that they were the pay which the Icelanders from the country received for working the fisheries for the owners of the boats and nets. Even the backbones of the fish are preserved and dried for fuel. On the evening of the 14th I dined with the Bishop, and there met Dr. Hjaltalim. The latter gentleman told me that eruptions in Iceland are always preceded by fine weather, which is very remarkable, as one would expect them to occur most frequently when the atmosphere was the lightest; that shocks of earthquake often precede eruptions, travelling from NE. to SW., or SW. to NE., and never in any other direction. The most terrible earthquake on record in this part of the world preceded the eruption from Kallugia in 1860. It thus seems that the primary cause of volcanic disturbances originates towards Jan Mayen and travels southward, or in the Azores and travels northward. Dr. H. also informed me that there formerly existed bays and fjords on the north and west coast which ships used to enter, but now are too shallow.

June 15th.—I took a walk along the coast, scrambling along the shore, which immediately by Reykjavick is rendered very rocky by an ancient lava stream upon which the town stands. It is a compact basaltic lava, but the whole of the stream is now covered with alluvial deposit. I took the bearings of the last eruption in Vatna Jökull, as seen from Reykjavick: the line cut Mosfell.

June 16th.—Wandered towards the lime-kilns outside the town. Near them were several heaps of carbonate of lime, which is obtained in considerable quantities from a mine beneath Mount Esjia; it does not, however, make very good lime, being of a very earthy character. The next day we paid a visit to the eider duck islands opposite Reykjavick. Here the ducks are greatly encouraged, and the owner of the farm receives as much as 600 or 800 dollars per annum from the sale of the eider down. In the evening we were plagued by a swarm of insects, half-gnat half-mosquitos. I afterwards saw a similar kind beneath Myrdals Jökull.

June 22nd.—Our horses arrived, concerning which very ordinary batch of ponies little need be said, except that they cost us sixty dollars each, worked very fairly through the summer, and sold for about fifteen to twenty dollars each when we had done with them, a result better than many other travellers obtained. While the work of shoeing was proceeding, we prepared our pack-boxes, and on the morrow we removed our camp to the Lax Á (Salmon River), some three miles from Reykjavick. The road lays over ancient lava fields, now scarcely discernible; we camped upon a beautiful piece of turf beside the river. In the evening Mr. Tompson came to look at his salmon boxes, and we assisted him to take out the fish. These boxes are let into the middle of dams placed across the river, so that the whole of the water has to pass through the boxes, into which the fish can get, but are unable to escape. We took from the boxes 450lbs. of salmon, and a beautiful sight it was to see those silvery monsters all alive, and looking fit for the table of a king.

June 24*th*.—It was not till 6 P.M. that the remainder of our chattels came from Reykjavick, accompanied by W—— and S——, but as I knew if we stayed where we were it would be the signal for our guide to take himself off to the town, from whence it would be hopeless to expect him for several hours in the morning, I decided, much against his will, to go on. C—— and I walked, for we agreed to give up our ponies for the present to carry baggage for the good of the community. One horse carried a sleigh I had brought from England for use upon the snows of Myrdals and Vatna Jökulls; but I soon found it was impracticable to carry it upon horseback, it knocked against rocks, would not be adjusted, and finally seemed to bid fair altogether to upset the poor little pony that carried it.

We fell in with a party of Icelanders, who were going our way, many of them were drunk. I would here say a word about drunkenness in Iceland. When this vice has been observed by many of our countrymen, who have only gone the usual round from Reykjavick, viz. Thingvellir, Geysirs, and Hecla, they have come to the conclusion that drunkenness is the Icelander's national failing. I am not going to say that I have not met a great number of drunken men in Iceland, still it is but fair to state that the Icelander in his home is not an habitual drunkard. When he gets intoxicated it is generally while he is on a journey, and consequently he is seen by all travellers; in other countries drunkenness is more of a hole-and-corner offence. Again, when Icelanders come to Reykjavick once or twice a year to trade, they are easier victims of temptation than those who are daily exposed to it. Having done their trading they leave the town in company with their friends, drinking first with one and then with another as they ride along; perhaps some of them have already taken more than was good for them before they started, and thus it is so many drunken men are met upon the roads immediately about Reykjavick. Granting all this, however, it is decidedly unfair and unjust to say that the Icelander, taking him all the year round in his own home, is an habitual drunkard.

Having travelled comfortably on for a few miles, a spare horse belonging to our guide took it into his head to rush to the front, stampeding the remainder of the horses; this resulted in the irons which fastened on one of the pack-boxes coming to grief, and the flinging of the box with full force on end against a lava block. This accident is a very common one, and it behoves travellers before starting to see that the irons which attach the boxes to the pack-saddles are perfectly secure. Leaving our guide and S—— to fix up the broken box, W——, C——, and I followed the rest of our horses, which we found in inextricable confusion about a quarter of a mile off. The sleigh was banging about against the lava blocks, and it finally became dislodged altogether. By the time we had set the sleigh to rights, and got the other horses together, S—— and Guthminder came up. We then commenced a long tedious march over a series of ancient lava streams, through slush and sand.

The sleigh at length became so unmanageable that I was obliged to hold the end of it up behind the horse. I never attempted to convey anything so utterly uncontrollable upon horseback before, except a sofa, and I do not know which was the worst of the two. We continued our by no means pleasant journey till 4 A.M., when we camped near Mosfell; our spirit lamp, *i.e.* stella lamp, did us excellent service, and as I lay down to rest, I formed a mental resolution not to carry the sleigh another yard, but to cook my breakfast with the wood of which it was made.

June 26th.—My first work was to carry into effect

my determination of the preceding night, and a good fire was soon kindled with the unpliant sleigh. Several trout were caught in a stream near our halting place, and in the evening we started for Thingvellir, following the same kind of rough road over old and weather-worn lava, interspersed with deep gulches, worn by the wash of streams through countless ages. After about five miles, C—— became ill, and was obliged to ride the spare pony. We ascended rapidly until we reached the height of 1,400 feet above the sea; a cold mist surrounded us, distorting the mountains around which it hung into the most fantastic shapes; it cleared, however, as we descended towards Thingvellir.

A descent of about 500 feet brought us to a plain grown over with herbage, and we were soon on the rough field of lava which has flowed into the Lake of Thingvellir, where the far-famed rift Almanna Gjá occurs. During this journey I was (as I had often been before) greatly struck with the little difference between the rate of progression of a man on horseback and a man walking. Sometimes, when a mishap occurred in our long line of pack-boxes, I drove on the remainder of the horses, while the rest of our party who were mounted stayed with the horse whose pack required attention, allowing me perhaps five minutes' start. I was always astonished at the distance made before the others could overtake me. At several points we caught sight of the Lake of Thingvellir, and by 3 A.M. we stood upon the edge of Almanna Gjá, gazing at the valley beneath us. Upon the north lay the crags of Arnanns' Fell, from which the winter snows had not yet melted, glistening in the light of the newly-risen sun; while the few soft clouds which had rested for the night upon them arose, and resuming their journey, soared into the fair beauty of the morning sky. Behind us was the dreary lava field and the western horizon still glowing with the sunset of yesterday; before us the green valley of Thingvellir, the Logsberg which for centuries served as a forum to the proudest of Iceland's ancestry, and the little church and parsonage of Thingvellir, with the River Oxerà winding down to the lake which bounded the valley upon the south. At our feet lay the black basaltic crags and rift of Almanna Gjá, a fitting sight to stir the ancient muse of Iceland's song; but though the softest morning breeze blew up the valley, no song broke forth in honour of the glories of that morning vision, and the only voice which disturbed the peaceful air was close behind me, giving undignified utterance to material requirements—"I say, let's get across and have something to eat!" We descended by an almost perpendicular path, crossed the river, camped, breakfasted, and got to sleep at 5 A.M.

June 26th.—We walked to the Logsberg: the sun was very hot, the thermometer at 12 o'clock A.M. rose in the shade to 69°, being a difference of 27° between night and day. The lava stream here was split throughout the valley by numerous crevasses of great depth, the bottom of which was often filled with the clearest water, containing small fish. It is to these chasms the Logsberg owes its security, it being surrounded, except at one little narrow point, by deep rifts, too wide for any one to jump (although there is a tradition of a condemned criminal having done so to save his life). It is thus rendered easily defensible by a few resolute men against a host; and it was on account of these natural fortifications that the ancient Icelanders chose it as a forum for the "Althing" to assemble upon. The lava abounds with a straggling undergrowth, which makes an excellent fire. I took some photographs of the scene around me, and then struck along the rift, passing a man who had come to make a bridge over the Oxerà for the king of Denmark, who was about to visit his island subjects. Passing to the north of the waterfall caused by the river falling over the cliffs of the Almannagia Gjá, I climbed up a small lateral rent over a great bed of snow, to the lava field above.

The accumulation of the winter's snow remains in these clefts all the year round.

I was particularly struck with the volcanic contour of the distant hills, so much resembling those around the Frith of Forth; for the features of a country's scenery, like the countenance of a man, usually pourtray the character.

Sunday, June 27th.—We remained in camp, enjoying lovely weather: we were 400 feet above sea level. We visited the clergyman, and examined the "measure stone," outside the church. (*See Plate.*) By this stone the ancient Icelanders regulated their measures. In the night the thermometer fell to 33°.

Monday, June 28th. — W—— busied himself in curing the head of a large trout he had caught and I crossed the river to have a look at that part of the Almanna Gjá exactly opposite our camp. The summit of the cliffs, as measured by my aneroid, was 600 feet above sea level, making the rift 200 feet in depth. From this point, perhaps, one obtains the best view of the valley and Lake of Thingvellir. The way the lava flowed into the valley is perfectly apparent; it has flowed from Skjaldbreith, and when the supply of lava ceased the surface of the great lava stream cooled, leaving the fluid matter beneath, to flow away into the deeper portions of the Lake.

The crust which had thus formed covered an immense hollow, and there no longer being any support for the superficial crust, a subsidence took place, forming two large lateral cracks; the one, Almanna Gjá, on the west, and Ravensrift on the east of the valley of Thingvellir.

About 3 P.M. we started for Geyser, and some time was spent in readjusting the burden of the horse that carried our whiskey; he was very obstreperous, and was repeatedly coming to grief. The road crosses the Ravensrift and ascends to the higher ground east of the valley of Thingvellir. Upon ascending from the valley, we for the first time saw the full extent of the Lake, the eastern portion, which had before been hidden by the hills, now coming into view. The lava here increases in its burnt and scoriaceous aspect, and as we approached Kalfs Tindr, an old volcano, the country was strewed with scoriæ and volcanic cinders. We here fell in with an Icelander and his son, who were carrying planks and stockfish on their horses, and it was wonderful to see how evenly they balanced those long and heavy pieces of timber, one on each side of the packhorse. The fish smelt abominably. At Kalfs Tindr we inspected some remarkable caves in the soft agglomerate[3] upon the side of the mountain, large enough to shelter sheep in winter; inside, the shepherds had carved some rude and curious designs. The ground now gradually descended. We remarked, as we passed a green patch of grass bespangled with the bright *dryas octopetala*, that we had not seen a daisy in Iceland. This is the more remarkable, as it grows profusely in the Faroe Isles; however, the *dryas octopetala* well takes its place, and though it has a more handsome blossom, is just such another unpretending bright cheery little flower, and well deserves the name of Iceland daisy. As we descended the valley we had a fine view of Hecla and the two lakes, Laugervatn and Apavatn.

This "darlr" was the most fertile I had yet seen in the Island; it contained many farms of the better sort. We here came upon a bright scarlet flower with a strong smell of heliotrope, but none of us knew its name. The steam from the boiling springs in this valley is observable a long way off; they principally occur around the Lake Laugervatn (warm water). We were soon camped in comfort upon a lovely soft piece of turf by the side of the Lake, with an occasional whiff of sulphuretted hydrogen to remind us we were in a volcanic country.

June 29th.—I paid a visit to the boiling springs upon the west side of the Lake. There are several of them, varying in size and temperature; most of them are intermittent, flowing and spouting at intervals of a few seconds; the temperature of some is at boiling point, but I have no doubt the apparent ferocity with which many of them bubble up is owing to the discharge of gases from below, rather than from any increment of superheated water. Many small springs rose out upon the margin of the Lake, emitting a frying sound, and a strong sulphureous smell. Close to the largest of the springs was a small patch of ground full of tiny holes, through which an aqueous vapour was continually rising, depositing a thick sublimation of what appeared to be alum and borax: the specimens I procured were afterwards lost. In one of the springs we boiled half a ham. These springs deposit no sinter, but a kind of black, earthy conglomerate: the taste of the water resembles that of Wiesbaden. The Lake itself curiously illustrates the relative specific gravity of hot and cold water, the surface of the water being in many places very warm, and at the depth of a foot very cold. After breakfast I ascended the mountain behind our camp, to the NW.; down its sides has flowed a very sharp and scoriaceous lava, while huge rocks of a hard blue basalt protruded in many places. I found a few volcanic bombs, and several masses of a light-coloured stone, as large as a man's head; they were too hard to be broken with a hammer, and when struck gave out a sound like clink-stone.

At our next start the first few miles were a continual series of mishaps, the guide mistaking the way, and several boxes breaking down. On reaching the Bruar Å, Guthminder was hopelessly at fault, and we had to retrace our steps over a very rough road; then came a breakdown, with a general stampede of the horses, and we were obliged to camp for the night, while the guide searched for a smith to mend the broken packsaddle.

June 3rd.—Our guide returned at 4 A.M., and immediately went to sleep; shortly afterwards two men made their appearance, and rousing Guthminder we set to work to mend the saddle. One of the men assured me he had a smithy, and that he could mend and strengthen the irons at the back of our packboxes. We agreed to wait for the repairs, considering that to have things put to rights was economy of time. But we were disappointed in our workman; he returned with the hooks I had given him as a pattern, and they were no stronger than before; so we set to work to do the repairs as well as we could ourselves.

Thus we lost a whole day, though I must say it was pleasantly passed. I went in search of W——, who had gone fishing in the Bruar Å: the river runs over a stream of blue basaltic lava, a large fissure which draws off the greater part of the water, leaving the rest very shallow, though rapid: this chasm is spanned by a bridge, which renders the crossing of the Bruar Á a matter of the greatest ease. There are several rifts in the lava over which the river flows; they lie immediately in the bed of the stream, and are filled with water, the clear depth of which is strongly suggestive of glacial ice: they would be very awkward places to fall into. W—— had caught some fine trout, and he returned to camp and cooked them for supper. This river also abounds in ducks, and its banks with plover and curlew. After supper I gave the horses some salt, which is a good thing to prevent them straying from camp; this artifice is much practised by the frontier-men of America; my adoption of it greatly amused the Icelanders. We started early next morning for Geyser, and three hours brought us to the plain in which these remarkable springs occur. A high wind was blowing, filling the air with dust and sand, blinding one; the air and clouds were dark with the light soil they held in suspension. These high winds, which are so frequent in Iceland, must rapidly and materially alter the face of the country, for the soil is a light sandy loam, and perhaps over an area of ten square miles some hundreds of tons may be in motion at the same time. We found two Englishmen camped at Geyser, and we lost no time in pitching our tent close to theirs. After refreshment I visited several of the springs, to see if any marked alteration had taken place since my former visit. I noticed some of the springs, especially Blazer (in which visitors generally cook), were rapidly becoming choked with the deposit of fiorite upon the upper part of the sides, where the water was the coolest. These springs are of great beauty; two large pools of the clearest boiling water, when the surface is unruffled by the wind, reflect from the more shallow parts a lovely azure, which deepens in tint, until it passes away into the black depths which lead down into the bowels of the earth. The walls and sloping bottom are of pure white fiorite, which in many places forms fanciful incrustations, clothed in ethereal blue, sometimes passing into pink, but the depth and character of the colour reflected seemed greatly to depend upon the state of the weather. I ascended the hill to the west of Geyser, in order to examine some remarkable ridges in the rock, apparently dykes, which stood out like walls from the face of the rock. These ridges are exposed by the splitting and falling away of the rocks, which are of a highly fissile nature, leaving these protuberances, like sheep walls upon the side of the mountain; their constitution is more compact, but they are to all appearance the same character of rock as that which surrounds them. There had been no alteration in the rocks they seem to penetrate, and I could not determine whether they were dykes or not. I had noticed large masses of sinter lying high upon the hill, and as they could not have been formed by water from the springs beneath them, it is probable the whole hillside must at some time have been perforated with boiling springs; indeed, there are two old worn-out geysers a short distance up the hill which in days gone by I doubt not were the counter part of those lower down ;* but they gradually committed suicide, by closing up their mouths with deposits from their own waters, as the springs beneath are all doing at the present day. The sinter upon the hillside occurs mostly in beds, in many places cut by mountain-streams, which flow only in rainy weather. Embedded in these I also found a number of spherical nodules; some were lenticular in shape, and all somewhat resembled volcanic bombs. I believe them to be formed from fragments of rock, or indurated mud, ejected and swallowed again and again by these ancient geysers, amongst the sinter of which I found them, and their rounded

---

* One of the most curious phenomena of this district is the different level of the various springs, which ranges to sixty feet.

form was most likely occasioned by attrition against the basin and sides of the springs, until some eruption more violent than usual flung them beyond the vortex of the funnel, into which they had before been continually redrawn.

July 2nd.—Weather had cleared, and we all hoped Great Geyser would spout, for it is a noteworthy fact that eruptions are the most frequent during fine and calm weather, thus following what appears to be the general rule of volcanic action in Iceland. I collected a number of very beautiful silicifications of grass, sticks, and other substances. Not forgetting the comforts of the inner man, we had brought with us ingredients for a plum-pudding: I have no doubt it was the first ever cooked in Geyser. It turned out very well, and was artistically served in flames of whiskey. Whether it was to repay us for the liberty we had taken of boiling our pudding in him, and then eating it under his nose, I cannot say; but just as we were in the middle of the first helping, Geyser commenced thundering and thumping, as though sledge-hammers were beating the earth's crust under our feet. We all sprung up, expecting to see Geyser in full play; but it was a false alarm: he boiled over, emitted a great cloud of steam, and then sank quietly to rest, a few inches only below his ordinary level. After supper we stirred up

VIEW OF ALMANNA GJÁ, WITH MEASURE STONE, FROM DOOR OF CHURCH AT THINGVELLIR.

Strokër in the usual way, by throwing down a quantity of stones and turf; and in about half an hour we witnessed a very fine display of this hydraulic popgun. The stones and turf being flung down the shaft of the spring, the water, which was then about fifteen feet below, began to boil apparently with an increased ferocity, and it rose slightly. There was no very perceptible difference in the aspect of the spring for thirty minutes, and we had just given up all hopes of exciting it, when a column of muddy water rose from the tube, perhaps, 120 feet, flinging up the stones and turf with which we had loaded it to a great height: it continued to play for twenty minutes. I learn from many other people who have recently visited Geyser, that Strokër kept them waiting an hour before he would perform a much longer period than he required for preparation in 1871; it may therefore be that he is getting worn out, or, in other words, the aperture which has to be blocked up, to allow the steam to generate below sufficiently to produce an eruption, is becoming enlarged, and is more difficult to close.

July 3rd.—The travellers we found encamped here when we arrived, thinking they had waited long enough for Geyser, departed. In the evening a magnificent eruption occurred; after a few convulsive throes, and without any long preliminary warning, grand columns of water rose, probably to the height of 200 feet. The great beauty of these displays arises from the purity of the water, and the immense amount of steam evolved during the eruption. Some stones which we had thrown in in the morning were ejected. We noticed that when any of the larger springs were disturbed, all the springs in the plain of Great Geyser gave off an increased amount of steam, showing that a sympathy existed between them.

July 5th.—A wet day. I collected a number of silicifications, and visited all the springs around Geyser: they almost all deposit a somewhat different sinter, which, like the differently coloured mud-springs, occurring as they do in such close proximity to each other, have greatly surprised many visitors. It is easily explained, by their water passing through variously constituted strata, in its passage from the heated source below to the surface of the earth, thereby dissolving the constituent parts of the rocks, which are soluble in their heated waters, and in cooling precipitate a deposit varying according to the nature of the rocks through which their course has laid. I purposely omit any lengthy description of these remarkable phenomena; people are too apt to consider them the chief objects of interest in the Island, and having seen them, have eyes for little else; they are, however, but secondary symptoms of volcanic activity, and though intensely interesting as curiosities, are not to be compared with the grander manifestations of volcanic force amid the volcanoes and snowy "Jökulls" in other parts of the Island, nor will time spent in watching them so amply repay the traveller, as will an examination of the centre of Iceland and its "Jökulls."

July 6th.—To-day we started for Rhuni, on the road to Hecla. As we left the plain of Geyser, the mountains to the W. arrested the attention of us all. The dark rocks rose to the height of over 1000 feet, veined and mottled with bands and patches of snow; the lava upon the sides looked as if it had flowed but recently; and, notwithstanding the great distance from us, every storm-shattered rock and rugged turn in the mountain stood out clear and distinct in the morning light. About half-way between the Geyser and the river Hvitá, we rode along the side of a tremendous ancient lava-stream, at one point displaying in the centre of the terminal wall peculiar basaltic formation. At first sight it appeared as if the columnar basalt had been formed by a different lava-stream from that which covered it, and that the basalt in turn overlaid a third stream; but I believe such was not the case, as there was no trace of scoriæ between what in such cases would have been the divisional surfaces of the streams; the base and slope of the stream, however, was much covered with alluvial deposit, disintegrated rock, and some undergrowth. We crossed the river Hvitá (White River) about 2 P.M.: it is a broad, deep river, running with a swift current, rising at the foot of Lang's Jökull, and discharging its waters into the sea at Errybakki. We and our luggage were conveyed over in a boat, while our horses swam; in doing this they showed considerable sagacity. The first batch of our goods, with C—— and S——, being ferried over, the horses were all led out into the stream, and driven forward with shouts and stones: they evidently knew what was expected of them, and they at once struck out for the baggage they saw on the opposite shore. We were now obliged to hire another guide, for without one who was well acquainted with the road, we could never have found our way through so rude a country. Our road was over the surface of an old lava-stream, through a series of deep gullies, some of which were sixty or seventy feet in depth. It was night before we reached Rhuni, where we camped.

July 7th.—We visited the provost-priest, who resided there. He entertained us very hospitably, and showed us his church: it contained a painting of our Lord's Supper over the altar, and a curious bronze plate, round which was inscribed the word RATHEWISTINBI; this, the clergyman informed us, no one had been able to translate: but Dr. Leitner, who saw the inscription a few months later, has since interpreted it.* We were also shown some beautiful carving done by the pastor's father, who had accompanied Thorwaldsen, the famous sculptor, to the north of the Island. When we left, the priest kindly sent his servant to accompany us to the River Thorsà. Immediately after leaving Rhuni, we passed a small warm spring which gushed from the mountain. Our way was over a very rough country, picturesque in the extreme, but exceedingly trying to the horses; I was on foot nearly the whole way, our horses being so heavily laden, but at the slow pace we were compelled to travel, it was scarcely so fatiguing as riding. Before reaching the Thorsà, we passed what may be almost designated a village of sheep-pens, which led one into another. Guthminder told us it was here the farmers sorted out their sheep in the autumn. He said that in September some 17,000 sheep were collected there, and that each farmer selected his own sheep, and penned them

* *Rathe wis tyne bi*, "Success be with thee." He conjectured it to be a baptismal font, that had come from Lubeck, between the 11th and 16th centuries, and that the figures upon it represented the salutation of Gabriel to Mary.

into one of these small pens. When we reached the Thorsá, we parted with the servant of our friend the provost. At this point a lava-stream from Hecla crosses the river, forming a series of rapids. The Thorsà rises at the western base of the Vatna Jökull, and empties itself into the sea a few miles to the SE. of the mouth of the Hvtá. Thorsà means Thor's River. We crossed it in the same way as we did the Hvità, and a girl, riding astride on a barebacked horse, guided us to Storruvellir. We travelled over sand and lava, which had been erupted by Hecla, occasionally emerging upon portions of the grassy plain which had not succumbed to the devastation which Hecla had spread upon the surrounding country, or upon ancient lava, now covered with alluvial deposit, and grown over with grass, through which the higher crop of the buried lava streams protruded. On our arrival at Storruvellir, we found the clergyman had gone to Reykjavick; so we camped near a small stream. The next day, not being astir early enough to ascend Hecla, I inspected the lava-stream which had flowed almost to the farm of Storruvellir. It is a compact lava, containing small crystals of feldspar and olivine; the surface in many places is covered with sand and grass, through which hummocks of lava, and the general waxy-looking scoriæ so peculiar to many of the ancient

Icelandic lava-fields, were observable. W—— caught some trout with very red-coloured flesh, but they were scarcely as good eating as those of Thingvellir.

July 10*th*.—A wet day, and Hecla was entirely obscured by clouds, well deserving her name, which means "cloak." Having suffered for some days with acute inflammation of the right eyelid, I was compelled to remain in tent and doctor it.

July 11*th*.—The weather being somewhat improved, I bandaged up my eye, and we set out for the mountain. We reached the little farm of Gastolœker about midday, passing over several lava-streams and tracts of sand and ash: here we stopped to drink coffee, and then proceeded, with the farmer as our guide, to ascend the mountain. We crossed the river Sola, which takes its name from the Sola (i. e. *Solan forso*). Before the eruption of 1848, the waters of this river abounded with fish. The farmer said none had since been caught; so I suppose they all then perished. We ascended on horseback to the termination of an arm of the lava-stream of 1848, a height of 900 feet. The stream has descended at this point at an angle of about 30°; the surface is very rough, and is covered with scoriæ, and masses of harder, stony lava, which probably welled up through the interstices: this lava has flowed in a very compact stream, sometimes resembling in the distance a huge caterpillar; although it spreads out in many places to fill up little valleys and declivities in the side of the mountain, where it is tossed about in huge black cindery waves, assuming all conceivable shapes and fantastic forms, and terminates in an accumulation of scoriæ, clinker, and *débris*, which formed a bank forty feet high at the termination of the stream. We passed on to the SE. over a thick bed of loose black sand, which covers a lava-stream, and makes dangerous holes for the horses. On our right was a fine specimen of a cinder cone, which we afterwards visited. We followed up the side of some remarkably round hills of sand and ash, which had been rounded by the action of the snow and weather. The snow which covers all these mountains in winter, as it melts in spring and summer, moves slowly down where the sides of these sand-hills are steep, rounding the soft, loose sand very smoothly and evenly; it both melts and moves in these hills the more readily, owing to the heat which is absorbed by the black sand. We left our horses at 2,400 feet; and there I gathered several cinders red as a brick. We again followed the lava-stream of 1848, which in many places was covered with patches of snow. My bad eye now became very troublesome; I had to bandage it with a large handkerchief, which almost obscured the vision of the other. The mist was fast falling, and encumbered with instruments and mackintosh, the work was none of the easiest. We passed several masses of white, hard rock, which when struck gave out a submetallic ring : I believe they must be some grey, stony varieties of obsidian. The lava had here poured down the steep incline in a thin stream, but we could see only a few feet on account of the fog; around us were great lumps of lava, which appeared like gutta-percha, passing at some places almost into obsidian. We were now 3,600 feet high, and we finally left the main body of the lava—which was now lighter and of a more porous nature—for the snow, which still lay very thickly upon the mountain. The fog had increased to blackness, and it was snowing fast, and I was nearly blinded when I reached the summit, or rather the crater of 1848. The top of the mountain was covered with snow, and the craters were completely blocked up, though a circular hole in the crater of 1848 had been thawed out by its heated exhalations. As it was utterly useless to continue any longer in this very uncomfortable situation, we descended, running down the snow slopes at a very rapid rate. Our guide eventually got off the track, and so when we had descended below the thickest of the fog, we found we were too much to the NW., and were obliged to clamber along the side of the mountain. After a most excruciating scramble over lava and snow, which was bad enough for a man possessed of all his faculties, but still worse for one almost blind, we at length reached the horses, which, I dare say, were not sorry to return to their pastures below. On our way down, we stopped to examine the cinder cone before referred to. The crater of this cone was 100 feet deep, and the side sloping at an angle of 60°: the bottom and sides were covered with patches of grass. We descended to the farm of Gastolœber, where I learnt that the eruption of last year from the unknown volcano in Vatna Jökull appeared from that point to be situated in a line directly NE. of Hecla.

July 12*th*.—Remained in camp with acute inflammation of the left eyelid, and the right much overstrained and weakened. The next day, feeling some improvement, and being exceedingly anxious to press on, we started for Breitherbolstad. Having now dispensed with two of the pack-boxes, we were all enabled to ride. Our way was over a sandy waste, in many places white with small pieces of pumice-stone which had been showered down from Hecla. Perhaps the most remarkable feature of the ride were the huge masses of sand and alluvial matter which stood isolated in all conceivable shapes upon the plain, and capped for the most part with a thick coarse herbage ; these were all that remained of a once thick soil of sandy loam, now almost entirely carried away by the rain and the sand storms of ages, leaving but these outrageously distorted masses to tell of the wondrously rapid change wrought in the face of the country by the wasting and degrading influences of the Icelandic climate.

After crossing the river we ascended to the higher ground, which commanded a glorious view of the plain of Hecla and the surrounding mountains, cutting them off, as it were, from the more eastern portion of the Island. The Plain of Hecla, now lying behind us, is the most fertile plain in Iceland, and contains more farms than any other. One great peculiarity of the sandy and barren portions of these plains, is the multitude of apparently water-worn pebbles with which they are strewn ; but the rapid shifting of streams, the great rainfall, and, though last not least, the attrition of the small sandy particles which are continually being blown along their faces, no doubt explain their appearance. All these plains which border the south of Iceland terminate in low flat shores, and it is quite probable that at some remote period the coast line was much farther inland than it is now; but although I made the most particular inquiries, I could gather no evidence of the sea having encroached or retrograded upon the south coast during historical periods.

The high ground on which we stood also afforded us a grand view of the snowy heights of Eyjafjla, Myrdals, Godalands, and Tindr Fjalld Jökulls. Of all the mountains I have seen, I think Hecla presents the most eccentric variety of form, if viewed from different aspects. From some points it appears like a single-coned volcano, resembling a conical blast furnace, with its steep sides sloping off to the plain upon which it stands; from others its three cones are perfectly visible, and it appears like a mere continuation of the neighbouring mountains. From the position we were now in, its true character and form were entirely lost, and the mist that enveloped its summit greatly assisted the transformation, cutting off, as it were, the upper part of the mountain, and causing the remaining portions to appear as if they supported a tableland of considerable magnitude. Right well does Hecla deserve its name of "The Cloak," or more properly perhaps "The Cloaked," and it would be no great stretch of imagination to suppose that cloak a magician, which transformed the wearer according to the disposition of his garment.

We arrived at Breitherbolstad by 11 P.M.; there

VIEW OF LOGSBERG FROM THE BACK OF FARM AT THING-VELLIR, WITH ARNANN'S FELL IN THE DISTANCE.

we for the first time noticed clover, which grew in rather large quantities. This was the small white kind, which grows profusely throughout the fertile portions of these southern plains.

Breitherbolstad is said to be one of the best farms in this part of the Island, and is in every way by far the best I ever visited while in the country. This belongs to a clergyman, and both he and his wife were most kind and hospitable : and if their countrymen would take a lesson from their domestic arrangements, the sanitary and social condition of the people in general, and their homes, would be much improved. We camped in front of the church : the churchyard gave as much evidence of careful attention as many others throughout the Island did of neglect.

July 14*th*.—By midday we left Breitherbolstad, crossing the river Maka Fljot, which is broad, deep, and rapid, and at certain seasons of the year is all but impassable. It rises in Toffa Jokull, and is fed by the rivers of Godalands and Eyjafjalla Jökull, and flows, in many arms, like so many distinct and separate rivers, through the level sandy plains towards the sea, enclosing a considerable tract of land. The course of these arms is continually shifting, leaving their old courses high and dry; this shifting is occasioned by the great variation in the volume of their waters, the immense amount of sand they hold in suspension, and the great accumulation of *débris* brought down by floods from the mountains. As we rode along we noticed a great number of round and oval balls of yellow sandy conglomerate, which had been rounded by the stream, and now looked very much like plum-puddings.

When we had crossed the river, on our left hand rose high cliffs of basalt and sandy conglomerate, over which rushed a great number of mountain streams, creating an abundant verdure upon their precipitous sides.

We fell in with a party of haymakers: the women were riding cross-saddle upon pads of such size, that they must have been, to say the least, inconvenient. By nightfall we reached Holt, where we camped.

July 14*th*.—Our course still lay along the plain, bordered by the sea on the south, and the magnificent cliffs, rising in many places to several hundred feet, on the north. The sun was shining brightly, and for the first time we observed considerable mirage, not only upon the horizon but upon the intervening plain; the appearances were principally like uncouth shapeless masses, though occasionally of familiar objects, and they were often raised in the air though not inverted. A few miles from Holt we passed a large cave in the conglomerate, of such magnitude, that from time immemorial it has been used as a court-room, and is at the present time used as the court-room of the "sysel." Our next object of interest was Scogar Foss. This is a grand waterfall, about 200 feet in height; the body of water is very considerable, and it continues to fall in a continuous series of sinuous fold (as W—— said), resembling the Stabbach. It displaces a vast amount of air in its descent, and the spray rising from it makes a near approach a matter of a wet skin, unless one wears a complete casing of waterproof. In connexion with this waterfall there is a legend of a coffer of gold, supposed to be sunk in the pool into which the water of Scogar Foss falls; but like many other legends, it has made itself perfectly safe from verification, by locating the treasure where it is quite certain no one will ever seek it. Scogar Foss, like most other waterfalls, has its own special characteristic, which is the impression it produces in the mind of the beholder of the wonderful momentum of a falling body.

We halted at the farm and parsonage close by, to refresh ourselves with coffee; and then, accompanied by the guide we had taken with us from Holt, we set out for the Jökull Sá.

The road here runs parallel with the glaciers which

lie between the Myrdals and Eyjafjalla Jökulls, and the cold atmosphere which envelopes these immense masses of ice and snow was very perceptible; large blocks of conglomerate and basalt, evidently brought down by the glaciers, and scratched and furrowed in their course, lay stretched upon the barren plain.

It was evening when we arrived at Jökull Sá: its waters were now rather low, for, like most of the other rivers, it is purely a glacial stream, and in warm sunny weather, at midday, is very difficult to cross. We journeyed on to the farm of Steig, passing the abruptly rising hills of Petrsey that rose upon our right, looking like rocky islands, which doubtless they once were, when the sea covered the plains upon which they stand. We ascended the grassy hills behind Steig, and camped at the foot of Burfell.

July 15th.—In the morning we separated, as W—— wished to go fishing, and I was desirous of visiting the Gœsir Tindr (Goose Mountain), and also of seeing what the environs of Myrdals Jökull were like, for the climbing of that Jökull was the next piece on our programme. The rest of our party did not care for so long an excursion. I first ascended Burfell: this, like the surrounding mountains, is composed of basaltic, sandy conglomerate, with masses of basalt protruding from the summit in eccentric-looking stacks, much weather-worn and split.

I then took the bearings of Gœsir Tindr as it appeared upon my map, and struck a line over the intervening hills towards it. In the glens and valleys between these hills are excellent pastures for sheep, flocks of which inhabit them.

Large slabs of yellow and red agglomerate may be seen in the watercourses, protruding from the sides of the hills, surrounded by beds of disintegrated rock and fragmentary *débris:* many of the rocks were glaciated, and the soft agglomerate was often furrowed very deeply.

From the bed of one of these streams I also gathered several fragments of pitchstone. I arrived at the base of Gœsir Tindr, which lies at the foot of Myrdals Jökull, at 12 A. M., and upon reaching the summit my aneroid registered 2,750 feet above sea level. The mountain commands a splendid view of the country towards the sea, and of the adjacent mountains. Gœsir Tindr is, I imagine, an old crater, from which, however, there appears to be no regular lava stream; but I noticed ash and a few pieces of vessicular lava in the immediate vicinity. An elliptical depression of perhaps 60,000 square yards is surrounded by almost perpendicular cliffs, the lowest part of which is 200 feet, and the highest

500 feet from the bottom of the depression. These cliffs are formed of agglomerate: two-thirds of the depression is occupied by a lake fed by numerous small streams which flow from Myrdals Jökull. From this lake commences the river Hafrsá, and the point where the stream finds exit is the only spot which breaks the continuity of the cliffs I have just described. Upon the highest point I rested to enjoy the view. Behind me, to the north, were the snows of Myrdals Jökull; around me, clusters of inferior eminences, together with ridges of hills, and rivers which had cut for themselves deep channels through the mountain's sides. The Hafrsá in particular had cut a cañon so deep and dark, that although its course was perfectly visible from the top of Gœsir Tindr, nothing could be seen of the river itself except the rivulet which started from the lake beneath me; beyond all lay the sea, with the whole of the coast line, its bays, fjords and prominences spread out before me like a map. Embosomed in the hills were many tiny lakes, similar to that of Gœsir Tindr, though most of them were larger. I descended into the depression below, and found the shore of the lake was black sand, with many boulders, some of which seemed somewhat dissimilar in nature to the adjacent rocks; but it was clouding over and getting on towards the

afternoon, so I commenced the descent, following the baby Hafrsá from its source. This river was soon joined by numerous tributaries, and I climbed the hills which shut it in upon the east, in order to avoid a great irregularity in its course. Upon meeting it again, lower down, it was a glacial river of no inconsiderable dimensions. I again descended to its bed and pursued my way along the eastern side. The stream now ran through one of the grandest cañons I ever saw, and was shut in on each side by perpendicular cliffs, whose snow-capped dizzy heights abounded in rifts and ledges, where the raven and the eagle had constructed their unmolested eyries.

After plodding along the river for about half a mile, I came to a spot where my progress was checked by a perpendicular wall of rock, whose base was washed by the river, which had now assumed the shape of a very ugly glacial torrent. I did not at all relish the idea of crossing the savage-looking river, whose dirty waters concealed its depth, and the force of whose current was moving pieces of rock of some magnitude, especially encumbered as I was with a heavy pilot coat, my capacious pockets full of mineral specimens, several valuable instruments upon me, and a geological hammer in my hand; but it had to be done, and there was no help for it, for I could not mount into the now cloud-covered hills, to wander about perhaps all night, vainly endeavouring to find my way home. I saw the current was very strong, and the water most likely over my waist; so taking up as large and heavy a stone as I could carry, I waded in, first up to my knees, then up to my waist, when I found I could scarcely stand—I tottered, slipped into deeper water, and the next instant was borne down the stream at the rate of an express steamer on the Mississippi. Down, down the gorge I went, almost powerless, bumped against blocks of stone, swept through eddies and rapids, sometimes in shallow water; but I could not rise, owing to the weight of my coat, &c., and then, again, I was in the deeper parts of the river. Presently I was washed against one of its sides, which rose in a high wall of agglomerate, and which had been hollowed out, by the wash of waters, into a series of low caverns, into which the river poured with relentless fury. To be carried under any of these recesses would have meant drowning in a very unpleasant manner; so, clenching my hammer, I exerted all my strength to keep myself from being sucked under that terrible wall. The fragments of basalt tore the flesh and skin from my knuckles, but I did not feel the pain at the time; and just as I was speculating whether the next thing I might be treated to might be a waterfall, the river turned, and I was carried into shallow water, upon a side of the river where, luckily, there was space enough for me to walk; here I scrambled out, without having sustained much damage, save bleeding hands, bruised knees, a lost cap and a thorough drenching. My clothes were now very heavy, and my progress slow. A little lower down I had to cross the river again, but at a part where it was divided into two streams, and so was more easily forded. Sometimes I had to climb along the face of the cliffs, and sometimes I was able to walk along the side of the river; at last I was again obliged to cross, where the stream had divided into several arms, so this was easily accomplished.

Glad, indeed, was I to reach the spot where I had left our camp in the morning; but my companions had moved on, leaving my horse under the charge of an Icelandic urchin, with a note which informed me they had gone on to Hethi. As it was raining hard, having given the homunculus a few skillings and mounted my horse, I rode quickly after the departed camp. I procured a guide from a farm I passed, and made my appearance in Hethi in time for my share of some good warm soup, which seemed indescribably palatable, and I discovered a piquancy in the concoction I had never before observed.

July 16*th*.—Still raining, as it had done all night; everything outside the tent was soaked, and a small stream was beginning to flow underneath the tent: for three days and nights there continued one incessant downpour, so heavy that we were compelled to remain in camp; everything we possessed was swamped, in the boxes as well as in the camp; pools of water collected underneath us, and my only coat had been hung outside to dry! The farm nearest to us was a poor one, and would not have accommodated us all, so we determined to remain as we were until the weather changed.

W—— and I occupied the windward side and door end of the tent, and the standing ground upon which we were camped caused all the drainage to flow in our direction; but I think even our companions will bear witness that we bore our trying position with equanimity. I made several experiments as to the amount of rainfall during the three days, by placing outside the tent a tin basin, three feet in circumference, and four inches in depth. The maximum time it took to fill was six hours, and the minimum four hours. Blank despair was upon the faces of every one as we shut out the pouring rain on Sunday night, July 19th, with but little hope for the morrow. I had been wet through over seventy hours, and was beginning to get accustomed to it; for, strange as it may be thought, it is just as easy to get accustomed to being wet through as to anything else, for as soon as the sensation of having wet clothing always in contact with the skin ceases to be novel, a reaction seems to set in, which makes the humid warmth not altogether uncomfortable. I remarked, as I lay down, that I believed it would be a three days' storm, which, with a SE. wind, is very common in these latitudes.

Monday, July 20th.—Comparatively, a fine day: a strong wind from the east, but little sun. We were, indeed, in a pitiable condition, everything was as wet as if we had been passing the last few days in the lake, instead of on terra firma. We spent the greater portion of the day in turning out our boxes and drying their contents. I rigged up a long clothes-line with our seventy yards of alpine-rope, stretched between ice-axes and climbing-poles, and by evening I was enabled to have a look round at Hethi.

Hethi is a fertile depression of some eight square miles, embosomed in mountains, and environed by the precipitous sides of the adjacent hills, some of which run to the height of over 1000 feet: a lake, abounding with trout, occupies one-third of the depression towards the south.

Tuesday, 22nd.—Our guide appeared in the morning, saying he had been to Hoffdabrekka, and had seen a man who could guide us to Myrdals Jökulls; and that he had engaged him to come on the morrow, if the weather should be fine enough for the undertaking.

Wednesday, 23rd.—Still raining, though not so heavily. After breakfast I put on my waterproofs and started for the mountains which border the lake just mentioned, following the course of a stream which empties itself into the lake. I observed that where the water had cut through a bed of alluvial deposit of fifteen feet in thickness, it had exposed a thick stratum of agglomerate of black volcanic ash and sand. I also perceived fragments of hard basalt, which appeared as if they had been perforated by apholas; but, on closer inspection, I saw that the holes I had mistaken for the perforations of that animal were elongated vesicles occurring in a basaltic lava, some of which were filled with crystalline matter. The ground around the lake was very hollow, and the waters of various small streams entirely disappeared from sight, but were plainly audible in their course beneath; this makes me the more inclined to the belief that the subsoil lies on an ancient lava stream, for the sudden disappearance and reappearance of streams is a special feature in ground so located. The water frequently percolates into cavities and hollows, perhaps reappearing only at the termination of the lava stream, or where it can find no subterraneous channel through the interstices or hollows of the lava.

The bed of the lake was a fine black sand; upon its shores I noticed a species of entozoon, probably excreted by some animal or fish. I climbed up the highest surrounding cliffs, the sides of which were covered with loose pieces of basalt, fallen from the agglomerate of which these mountains are formed. I was struck (as I had often been before) with the regularity of the angular form in which these fragments occur. Towards the summit the rocks are of a lighter colour. I also observed many volcanic bombs and partially fused fragments of basalt embedded in the face of the rocks. The top of these hills was a sharp ridge, extending almost round the entire amphitheatre of hills encircling the lake, bisected at various points by rocky eminences. This ridge in many places was less than three feet wide, and as I walked along it I could see nothing but the densest fog above and below me. I stopped on one of the highest points, watching the wind which had now risen, chasing away the clouds of mist that kept boiling up beneath my feet. Soon the fog decreased in density, and a bright spot showed that the sun was struggling with the dense atmosphere above. This bright spot became encircled with concentric rings of light, which seemed to spread out and increase in size and brightness every moment, clearing, as it were, a path for the sunshine. I returned to camp and was glad to find a fine day below.

W—— had been fishing, and had caught two kinds of fish—one the natives call "blœker," apparently a kind of char, and the other "rauther," which resembled a sea-trout. As the weather now seemed likely to clear, we prepared for a trip to Katlugia; but our anticipations were not realized, for the next day looked anything but hopeful. So instead of starting for Katlugia, *en route* for Myrdals Jökulls, as we had proposed, S—— and I, accompanied by the farmer from Little Hethi (the next farm to Hethi), named Brenyolver, set out for Gœsir Tindr, as I wished to have another look at it. We rode up the hill to the north, and, after about an hour, we left our horses in a little valley where sheep were feeding, and proceeded. We were soon, however, enveloped in fog, and could see nothing of the formation of the depression before described. It is surprising, if these depressions are ancient craters, that there is not more lava visible around them; for, as it is, lava only here occurs in fragmentary forms. But when we consider how the rivers, varying in their course, wash away the surface of vast tracts,

GREAT GEYSER IN ERUPTION.

and as quickly recover them with detritus and sand—how stupendous debacles, bursting from time to time from the Jökulls, cover the plains and the sides of the mountains with the accumulated *débris* of ages—how the gentle streams slowly and surely eat away the soft friable agglomerates, depositing their disintegrated constituents in other places—how the heavy storms metamorphose the face of the land—how the fierce dry winds remove whole tracts of the loose, sandy soil—how whole syssels are laid desolate, and mountains formed and destroyed by sudden outbursts of slumbering volcanoes,—we begin to understand how rapid and almost incredible is the change which is going on in this country, and cease to wonder that, even if these lakes be craters, there are no traces now existing of their former activity. Again, nothing is more probable, if these lakes are craters at all, that they, like Katlugia, for lengthened periods, if not at all periods of eruption, gave out only scalding water, mud, and sand. Our guide informed us that there used to be fish in Gœsir Vatn, as he called the lake in the depression of Gœsir Tindr, but that now there are none. I could not learn the date at which they ceased to exist.

We returned to our horses, and after riding a short time, the fog increased in density, and by the uncertain course our guide was taking, it became evident he had lost his way. We wandered about for some time, and at length came to a dead stop upon the edge of a precipice, down which we could see nothing but fog, although we could hear water running below at a very great depth. We could do nothing but follow our guide, and we did so for about three hours, and were twice brought up at the same spot upon the edge of the precipice.

This walking in a circle was becoming monotonous, so, striking upon a small stream, I decided on following it down the mountain. Our guide, however, declared he could show us the way " all right." Taking off his coat, and muffling up his face, he twisted round and round, until he fell down perfectly dizzy : he laid for a few seconds, and then got up, saying he knew the way ; and as he proceeded to lead us in the direction in which the stream was flowing, we followed him. Before we had gone any great distance we caught sight of Hethi Vatn and were soon at camp. This getting lost within half an hour of our guide's home was quite inexcusable, for the character of the mountains was so marked that even in fog anyone who had travelled two or three times the same way ought never to be at a loss as to the direction. This plan of turning round is a common fancy among many of the Icelanders: they believe that by making themselves giddy they can at once find the north. All this trouble might have been prevented if I had taken my compass, but as we were going so short a distance, and with a guide, I did not think it would be required.

W—— still kept the fish department of our mess well supplied, and we found he had caught some magnificent trout; one of them weighed, I dare say, twenty pounds, but the largest of them were infested with a flat white-jointed worm, resembling the tapeworm, which in some parts penetrated the flesh.[4] The Icelanders said the fish were perfectly wholesome (but we could scarcely think so), and that the same worm likewise infested the cod. The same species of worm was noticed in fish by the American Government Expedition to the Yellowstone Valley. The Icelanders suffer terribly from tapeworm: the carelessness as to their food is no doubt the cause of it.

Friday 25.—The man had come to guide us to Katlugia; but the mist hung low upon the hills, and a determined drizzle had set in, so we decided that the trip was impossible. I started away, in spite of the weather, to see what I could of the mountains to the north; the rest of the party preferred remaining intent. I ascended the hills behind the camp, to the NNE., where the mountain had been denuded by a stream, now of considerable size, which was swollen by the rain; here was exposed, to the depth of 150 feet, a thick bed of fine black ash: this was deposited in a series of curved layers, the surface being rounded by the action of the water. At first I could scarcely account for this immense deposit, but a very probable explanation soon presented itself:—Supposing the surface of the country in the immediate neighbourhood to have been recently covered by showers of fine dust, from some volcano in the vicinity, nothing would be more likely than that, by the action of the wind, it would have carried it into such a hollow, which perhaps lay directly in its course, and into which a strong current of air might have been moving. 1,100 feet higher the mist became very dense, but at the height of 2,150 feet it was lighter, and disclosed the bare summits of the mountain I was upon. I followed along the brink of a precipice, and upon this I found some large masses of lava protruding through a thick bed of *débris,* and evidently of very ancient date. The mountain here shelved off at such an angle as to compel me to sit down in order to descend; but as I could see little before me, after sliding down a hundred feet or so, I was not surprised to find the side shelve off altogether, compelling me to climb along it under somewhat difficult circumstances. Great quantities of loose stone had accumulated, which my movements continually displaced, and sent with great noise into the gulf below. The position did not afford a very good opportunity for observation, but I noticed several large hard pieces of rock, which when struck sounded as though they were hollow; I also saw lumps of black glassy obsidian. Eventually, the angle of the mountain, much to my relief, decreased, and a slope of indurated snow, from which a stream of water was flowing, brought me to flat ground, but of what extent I could not see, owing to the mist. It had been my intention to strike for a conical hill, bearing NNE. from our camp, but it was now 3 P.M., and raining hard, with no probable chance of the fog clearing; I therefore gave up my intention, and having lunched under the lee of a rock, made a detour to the west and south towards home. I rambled on for some time, and followed the course of a stream, which was going my way, and had cut through the mountain; from its appearance it must sometimes assume very formidable proportions. Its water had worn away the agglomerate into all conceivable shapes—one, especially defined, appeared like a ruined lighthouse. The stream had brought down a great number of rocks, and some large masses of basalt particularly attracted my attention; they were very hard and brittle, and split off into thin laminæ; presenting a conchoidal fracture like that of flint, they would have made excellent weapons during the stone period.

I reached camp about 6 P.M. The weather had cleared, and the rest of my party had gone out fishing and shooting; so I took a walk to have a look at a party of haymakers, who were cutting and gathering in their grass. They were mowing, or rather chopping, with long straight-handled scythes, with short thin blades. The grass was not more than six inches long, very scanty, and grew in a hillocky swamp. Most of the grass I have seen in Iceland has been of the same description; it is generally cut, and then carried near the farm to dry. The labour of gathering in a winter's supply for a few horses is great, and requires both industry and perseverance. It was the family of my guide of the previous day who were at work here, and upon seeing me, they would not let me leave them without going to the farm and taking coffee. The farm was a very poor one; the front room was blocked up with a bed, and a large wooden weaving-machine. They produced a harmonicon (it is a favourite instrument in this part of the Island), and played a few tunes, thus showing their hospitality, though it was rather ill-timed, considering they were in the middle of their hay-harvest, and I was wishing to get back to camp; still I could not but accept it with gratification.

July 26*th*.—I was awoke by a dog, which had taken up his quarters outside our tent; he announced

START FOR KATLUGIA.

the arrival of the man from Hoffdabrekka, who was to guide us to Katlugia. We were soon up, and under weigh at 9 A.M. The weather seemed inclined to clear, though a mist was still hanging about the tops of the hills. We rode along the track to Hoffdabrekka, until we were level with the mountain Arnastakker, and then turned up a gorge to the north, up the bed of the river. Rocks of great height rose on each side, of the same character as those around Hethi. We rode for about an hour, then climbing up the eastern side, we reached a grassy plateau, upon which was pitched a tent belonging to some farmers, who had come there to cut grass. Here we drank some coffee, and hired a man to accompany us as far as it was practicable to ride, in order that he might take back the horses. We soon caught sight of the black, barren, sandy plain of Myrdals Sandr, the greater part of which has been formed by the volcano Katlugia. To the north was the snowy Jökull, and before us, to the east, the broad plain, whose black sands united in the distance with the purple sky. Again we followed the bed of a river, which branched off into two arms, one coming from the north, and the other from the west. We took the northern direction. The bed of the river rapidly narrowed, and it was not long before we came to a halt, before a good-sized cave, upon the west side of the stream; it was perfectly dry, and had often been the resort of shepherds. At this point we dismounted, and left in the cave our saddles and bridles, and took lunch. We then sent the man back with the horses, with instructions to hobble them upon the grass-land near his tent until our return. We made our way up the gorge, whose perpendicular sides rose sometimes to an elevation of four or five hundred feet: fanciful masses of agglomerate towered above us, in the form of turrets, pinnacles, and embattled walls, while numerous caves and rounded ledges showed plainly the way the stream had worn a path for itself down this long grand defile of threatening heights. Along the course of the stream were masses of rock, which had fallen from above, while many others seemed to totter in their giddy elevation, as if ready to join their companions below. The gorge terminated in a small "fosse,"[4] some forty feet in height: here the eye could follow the stream but a little way in its course along the gloomy rift through which it struggled. Now commenced a hard scramble up the precipitous sides of the ravine, over beds of loose and shifting pieces of rock, which had collected wherever the sides were not too steep for them to rest: this loose stuff is very tiring to climb, but is both easy and pleasant to come down. A little more hard work brought us to another cave, and as it was raining, we took refuge in it until the rain ceased. Upon resuming our journey, we crossed an incline of pebbly stones, upon which were masses of rock, bearing glacial scratches.

The most remarkable feature of our excursion now stood before us: it was a long and narrow strip of mountain called Errins Sandr. Upon the west it was cut off from the main body of the mountain by the stream before mentioned; in many places at the top it was scarcely three feet wide, while upon the east side an incline of some eighty degrees made it a narrow and dangerous peninsular of rock, girt upon either side with terrible precipices, one of which was 250 feet, and the other, I dare say, 700 or 800 feet deep. Our course lay over this apparently impracticable road, although our guide informed us it was the only assailable point. By means of this unpromising path, at the height of 3,300 feet above sea level, we reached a plateau which, sloping upwards, joined the high glaciers of Myrdals Jökull at 3,600 feet. The irregular surface of the plateau was covered with huge slabs of basalt and patches of snow. We went along the eastern terminal edge, bounded by a precipice of 300 feet, at the bottom of which the glacier swept like a frozen, stormy ocean, its icy billows—in places black with sandy moraine—

piled over one another, rifted and contorted with the force by which they were driven against the immoveable and seemingly eternal wall of rocks we stood upon; then, as if its fury had been spent, it stretched away in broader and more even waves into the misty distance far below us. Upon the opposite side of the valley was a black aggregation of rocks and ice, but the mist would not allow me to inspect it through my telescope. A slope of nevé, from which protruded numerous mounds of sand and ice, brought us to the Jökull. Our guide had never been so far as this before, and seemed very anxious to proceed. It was one of those hazy days that are a great deal better for mountain travelling than a scorching sun. W——, myself and the Icelander were in high spirits at the idea of an interesting scramble over a hitherto untrodden glacier; but the sight of the cold and dismal Jökull seemed to have quite a different effect upon our other two companions. They declared it was quixotic and foolhardy to go on. I had joined the rope to W——, myself and the guide, for I saw there was much snow farther on upon the glacier, but the others declined being attached, nor could I persuade them to move farther. Seeing, therefore, it was impossible to accomplish anything with our present party, we decided, somewhat reluctantly, to return.

It may be as well if we now cast a retrospective glance at the history and character of Katlugia. Katlugia has erupted no less than fifteen times since the year 900. The special characteristic phenomena attending eruptions from this volcano are the huge floods of heated water with which it from time to time has flooded the adjacent country. These issuing suddenly from the crater during periods of eruption have rushed down the mountain slopes, gathering up all pulverent and fragmentary accumulations, mingling together the aqueous and igneous ejectments in a most horrible and heterogenous confusion, and finally hurling themselves in vast volumes of agglomerate upon the plains below, filling depressions with a seething paste, and flooding extensive areas with scalding water. It has been explained that these floods have been caused by the sudden melting of the Jökull; but this seems scarcely to be satisfactory, since other mountains, uncovered by any icy accumulation, have exhibited similar phenomena. In 1631 several villages, amongst which were Torre del Greco, were destroyed by a torrent of boiling water, which burst from Vesuvius with the lava. In Sicily, in 1790, several fissures sent forth sulphur, petroleum, steam and water. The instances of water issuing from volcanoes in Iceland and many other parts of the world are very numerous.

It is quite probable that in the case of Katlugia immense volumes of water may accumulate from the gradual melting of its icy covering during long periods of tranquillity, and remain stored up in some huge subterranean reservoir until an eruption bursts their prison. But when we consider the vast extent of country that from time to time has been flooded by this volcano, these aqueous phenomena are scarcely to be accounted for by any sudden melting of the Jökull.

July 27th.—It was raining heavily, as it had done all night, and at midday it beat down with such violence, that we were compelled to forsake the tent, and seek shelter in the little farm. As there was only room for two of us, our two friends elected to ride to Vick, a much larger and better farm, upon the sea-coast, and W—— and I availed ourselves of the shelter at hand, and here we came to the conclusion that, for the furtherance of the purposes of the expedition, it was best to part from our companions. We, therefore, determined to hire two Icelanders, and start on our own account, as soon as the weather would permit of our doing so. We decided to camp upon the plateau at the edge of the glacier, from whence we should be able to make several excursions upon the Myrdals Jökull.

July 28th.—I rode over to Vick, and informed

BASIN OF GEYSER WHEN EMPTY.

our fellow-travellers that, weather permitting, we should start at 6 A.M. on the morrow, and that if they wished to accompany us they must hire Icelanders for themselves, so that we might not be hampered by their movements, in case they wished to turn back. The next day being wet, we could not proceed. Our friends, however, came over, and took leave of us.

During our stay with the clergyman in the little farm of Hethi, nothing could exceed the kindness and attention of himself and his family; though their house was a poor one, they were clean and tidy in their habits, and were an astonishing proof that cleanliness and comfort were not impossible even in an old-fashioned Icelandic house, and many of their countrymen who live in the new-fashioned farmhouses would do well to imitate the homely thrift and domestic hospitality of the good folks at Hethi. Our host kindly abandoned the best and downstairs apartment to us, some dozen people occupying the upper chamber. His daughters, who were perhaps the nicest looking girls we saw in Iceland, played the harmonicon, and the evenings (for we now had a few hours of night) were generally spent pleasantly, with all the inmates of the farm assembled to sing Icelandic songs, for which we in return sang English. The old national songs are generally monotonous, but many pretty Swedish airs are now popular.

July 29*th*. — W—— and I, accompanied by two Icelanders, one named Sigurd and the other Brenyolver, set out for Myrdals Jökull, taking with us rugs, instruments, and a great sheet of canvas, which had previously served for the flooring of our tent. We left our horses to graze upon the same hills as we had done a few days before. Our man, Sigurd, was young, short, and strong, the very personification of sturdy doggedness; Brenyolver was a man of fifty years, who talked a great deal of his mountaineering. Upon reaching the cave, I began to entertain great doubts as to the soberness of the latter; he declared he must drink some coffee before he proceeded, and was so impudent, that had it not been that I was determined to get all my things up to the foot of the glacier that evening, I should decidedly have sent him back. We commenced the ascent at 5 P.M., and I more than once entertained grave fears concerning Brenyolver, who carried the methylated spirit for cooking, lest he should fall and break his neck. We were very heavily laden, and I perspired profusely, although it was cold and rainy, much to the detriment of my matches, as I afterwards found. Brenyolver became more and more intoxicated, but I could not ascertain by what means, until I reached the plateau upon which our camp was to be pitched : he had lagged much behind, and upon going to find out the reason for his doing so, I found him seated upon a large stone, drinking the methylated spirit, which he was carrying. He was in a state of complete incapacity, and all that I could get from him, in answer to my exhortations to go on, was " *Mikid slimt fyrir gamlan Islanding,*" "Very bad for old Iceland man," which he reiterated in a plaintive voice, and at length began to cry. I took his load from him, and left him to himself. We camped about a quarter of a mile from the point whence I had determined to attack the Jökull, upon the edge of the plateau I have before described. Here we built up four walls of stones, and roofed them with the sheet of canvas we had brought for that purpose. While building the hut, a hail-storm burst upon us, the spherical little pieces of ice, as large as a good-sized pea, pelting us unmercifully. During the course of our operations our drunken servant came up, and lying down, at once went to sleep. We could see the rifted and thickly-crevassed glacier beneath us now, more plainly than we had done upon our former visit; and the black, indistinguishable mass we had previously noticed was evidently a small volcano, whose grim mouth gaped at us from the opposite side of the ice. By 11 P.M. night closed in. When the camp was fitted up, and the residue of the spirit put into the lamp, I found, to my dismay, that my waterproof (?) match-bag was wet through, and most of my matches were spoilt. We succeeded at length in getting a light, and cooked some lamb and soup; but the wind drove the rain, hail, and sand through the crevices of our habitation, and made our night's lodging anything but a bed of roses. Brenyolver awoke in the middle of the night, and mingled with the flapping of our roof his old cry of "*Mikid slimt fyrir gamlan Islanding :*" he groaned and rolled about, until I began to fear he was suffering from *delirium tremens*. The rain, which was falling fast, had found its way through our extemporized roof, and we were lying in sandy slush. Our surroundings were by no means agreeable. The storm increased in fury, and gust after gust seemed as though it would sweep us and our temporary abode away; and the idea of perhaps having to struggle with one of the dirtiest of dirty Icelanders, in a fit of delirium, upon the edge of a precipice, on such a night, was scarcely a thing to look forward to with anything like complacence. The night, however, passed away without such a realization of my imaginings, and the morning showed us the beginning of a stormy day.

Friday, July 30th.—Peering down the precipice, on the brink of which our house was built, the eye fell at once upon the glacier, black with volcanic sand; at every step was a dark rift, that seemed to unite the terrors of the volcano and glacier. On the opposite side of this ghastly valley was the little black crater, its grim, funnel-shaped sides of sand and ash catching the clouds that crept along the dark wreaths of detritus, which spread out from Katlugia in inky waves, mingling with the glacial ice and snow: huge cracks and snowy clefts extended upwards towards the high glacier and summit of Myrdals Jökull, now dim with gloom, presiding over all, and breathing from her icy lips a freezing breath. Standing there that stormy morning, looking into the gulf at my feet, made me almost think I was gazing into one of Dante's abodes for evil spirits, where they are tortured alternately by fire and frost. I cannot conceive any place more calculated to disturb the mind of any one at all inclined to be superstitious. I conferred with W—— as to whether we had not better dismiss our " gamlan Islanding," and seek another attendant, and in doing so acquire a fresh supply of matches. He fully concurred with me that it would be best to do so, and as he preferred inspecting the surroundings of our hut, and improving its construction, if the weather abated, to making another descent of the mountain, Sigurd, Brenyolver, and I returned to Hethi, where I obtained some matches, and a fine young fellow named Johan Magnaldson, the very counterpart of our attendant Sigurd. We loaded ourselves with a fresh supply of provisions and spirit, and set out on our return journey in the evening: a hurricane had been blowing all day, the hail and rain had increased, it was very foggy, and growing dark. Heavily laden as we were, it was as much as we could do to make any headway. It is needless to relate the many troubles of that awkward and severe struggle up the sides of that storm-wrapped mountain. I must say the Icelanders behaved remarkably well; the peremptory manner in which it had been necessary to act with Brenyolver evidently had a beneficial effect, and although it was as much as flesh and blood could do to climb the mountain in such a tempest, it was done without a murmur from either of them. I was anxious to push on to my companion above, who had now been left some fifteen hours alone. Upon reaching the plateau, the clouds were so thick and the storm so violent that we passed within fifty yards of the hut without seeing it, nor did we discover our mistake until we found ourselves confronted by the slopes of nevé, leading to the Jökull. We returned, following along the edge of the precipice by which our hut was located, and right thankful were we to see the figure of my friend, standing to welcome us to our now much improved abode. He had heard the sound of our alpenstocks against the rocks, and had come out to look for us. Our roof, by W——'s labour, was rendered almost waterproof, and the chinks and crannies being stopped up, it was less airy, and far pleasanter. Rude as it was, it was a haven of rest, which I appreciated more than I have often done the best accommodation in my native land; and having lighted a candle, as I stirred some soup over my spirit lamp, I warmly entered into the feelings of an Esquimaux, in his affection for his oily fireside. The light of our wax candle, a pipe, some of Stortridge, Lawton, and Deck's good Scotch whiskey, and a song, alternately in English and Icelandic, quite banished the memory of the toil and travel of the day, the terrors without, and the solitary waiting on the part of W——; creating upon the storm-blasted rock upon which we were perched a brighter spot than had ever laughed in the face of Katlugia. Our half candle went out, our songs ended, and our grog was consumed: the rain beat down more furiously than ever, and by morning sufficient water had found its way into our habitation to suggest the thought that Myrdals Jökull had regarded its intrusive visitors as creatures of an amphibious order in creation.

August 1st.—A dubious morning, but wind NW.; the only wind in Iceland with which one is certain of fine weather. After breakfast our first work was to enlarge and improve our shelter. I then took a few observations, and found the compass was seriously affected, the attraction varying sometimes within a few yards; but I made out Hatta to be SSW., and Haversey a trifle to the north of east, which would make Katlugia about five English miles due north. Our height was 3,500 feet. The thermometer registered 2° of frost in the night outside our tent. The ground immediately around us was strewed with fragments of basalt, and masses of it stood out in ledges from the side of the precipice. In a SW. direction, and at no great distance, was a perfectly conical mountain; but I could not find it had any local name. We stopped up all the crevices of our hut with moss, which grew abundantly in various places. At 11 a.m. there was a fine view of Orefa, Vatna, and Skaptar Jökull. Upon Vatna I could see two black, conical eminences, the Hagaungu Hujukur; but I could discover no signs of activity through my telescope. We set out from Myrdals Jökull at 12 a.m., and were soon plunged into a considerable depth of snow, which in many places concealed fissures in the ice.

I adjusted the rope as before. Immediately upon leaving the Fjall, I ascended to the NE., going round the valley below our camp. Our Icelanders, who had never before been upon a Jökull, behaved well, exhibiting no signs of fear, although they were passing for the first time in their lives some large and ugly crevasses. We ascended to the height of 5,500 feet, nearly the summit of the Jökull, up some steep snow slopes. From this point there was a glorious view of the surrounding country. Vatna, Skapta, and Orefa were now obscured by the clouds; and a strong NW. wind was raising large clouds of sand upon the plains to the east; but the Fjalls and the tops of Godalands and Merker Jökulls stood out clear and sharp in the cold transparent atmosphere. Godalands and Merker, with the mountain we stood upon, appeared to hold between them the accumulated snow of ages, but a small proportion had been allowed to escape their grasp to feed the numerous glaciers that fringed their snowy heights, and swept down in broad seas of ice to a much lower level than the last snow patch upon the Fjall beneath. Upon the summit of these mountains there was nothing but pure white snow, though the glaciers to the east and south were black with a sandy moraine; and they all three appeared to be smooth and rounded eminences, which, perhaps, beneath the deep covering of many a winter's snow, might have been conical. To the east lay a horseshoe-shaped valley, cutting into the centre of Myrdals Jökull, round which protruded black elevations of no great height. The sandy detritus upon the glacier had evidently all come from this direction. Could this be Katlugia? It was very unlike what I had pictured to myself of the yawning chasm, which had to account for all the devastation eastward. I had expected to find it in, perhaps, a state of solfatara: and it was not on the spot indicated upon the map. This was a valley choked with the sudden birth of an immense glacier within it, around which enormous cliffs of snow had risen, and appeared as though they had stood there for ages. It was so utterly different from what we had expected to find, that we at once dismissed the idea of it being Katlugia; remarking that doubtless it was a similar ancient crater, of much larger size. We made some sage comments upon the magnitude of ancient volcanic disturbances as compared with those of historic date; but we did not in the least recognise the fact that we were looking into Katlugia itself. We proceeded along the SW. and N. edges of the valley at these points, girt with slopes of snow, which were split up and divided into immense consolidated masses, where they descended into the valley, rapidly passing into the truer glacier, with which this depression is filled. In many places the glacier was fearfully crevassed and blackened, with commingled ice and sand. We returned to camp amid a storm of hail, the little globules of ice dancing around us, and glancing from the now frozen surface of the snow, were swept by the wind into bewildering wreaths and eddies. It cleared, however, by 11 P.M., and as the wind was NNW., there seemed every prospect of fine weather on the morrow.

August 2nd.—No one awoke till 8 A.M., although we had purposed starting early; but it was not surprising that our sleep was so deep and sound, considering the roughness of the two previous nights, and the hard work of the last three days. The index of my thermometer registered 6° of frost during the night.

Immediately after breakfast we set out for the Jökull. We ascended more to the west than before, as we wished to reach the top of Myrdals Jökull, and from there to determine which was really Katlugia. Owing to the heat of the sun, and the disturbing influences of our progress, the snow was continually shifting. This somewhat startled our Icelanders, as each shift formed a small crack, which disclosed pure white snow beneath, and emitted flashes of dazzling white light, which were very trying to the eyes. I may mention that we all wore snow spectacles on this and other occasions, and but for this precaution we should doubtless have suffered from snow blindness. We attained the summit of the Jökull at a height of 5,750 feet, a snowy valley separating us from Gotlands Jökull, upon the NW., and Merker Jökull more to the north.

The sun was intensely hot, and we now rested to take a few observations. The grim valley beneath our encampment now bore a very different aspect to what it did on the stormy morning when we first gazed upon it. Now there was a beauty in those dark waves and sable banks of sand, where before we could discover nothing but the terrible. The crater before us awoke a keen interest, instead of exciting a feeling of repulsion. The dread horseshoe valley, which seemed to penetrate to the very bowels of the mountain, appeared in all its symmetry of shape, light and shade beautifully blending amid its wild confusion; and its dark chasms were made darker than ever by the contrasted light. Oh, how circumstances alter the character and colour of the scenes through which we pass! We now descended into the huge reservoir of frozen matter lying between Myrdals, Godalanders, and Merker Jökulls. These reservoirs are almost environed by snowy eminences, from which various glaciers extend down towards the streams and rivers, which in their turn restore to earth the precious gift of water, which an all-creating Power has ordained, alternately to quench the thirst of arid lands, to swell the seas, to hang awhile in space, to fall in dew or rain, or else to be stored up, as in these inconceivably huge reservoirs of frost and snow. The magic word which the voice of all nature breathes in circulation proclaims the existence of a Creative Mind. Here, side by side, and in the same identity, have we the vivifying and destroying powers of nature. Look to the east, at that black, dreary waste of sand! It has all been caused by the unequal distribution of the elements of heat and water. Heat which, when equally distributed, restores from these frozen Jökulls the river and the streamlet; when unequally dispensed, produces the paroxysmal outburst of the slumbering volcanoes, which then belch forth a destroying flood.

We lunched with Esjiafjall Jökull due west, and as we were due north of Hethi, we came to the conclusion that the horseshoe-shaped valley (before alluded to), which was now to the east of us, could be none other than Katlugia. We continued our course to the north, intending to make for Milafellsandr; but at 5 P.M. a fog closed down upon us: our last bearings were Myrdals and Esjiafjall Jökulls, SSW. It soon began to snow, and we could not prevail upon our Icelanders to strike for Milafellsandr, which could not have been very far distant. We rigged up a shelter with macintoshes spread upon ice-axes, and took some refreshment. In the course of the evening the snow ceased, and the fog cleared as the sun set, at about 10.30 P.M. As the fog was dispersing, a beautiful fogbow appeared to the SE. A rainbow-coloured cross, partially encircled between two segments of a circle, was visible for, I should say, a quarter of an hour. We felt this to be a very interesting incident in our day's work, compensating for much of our toilsome travel, for it was a very beautiful object.

We did not reach Myrdals Jökull till the sun had set: a sharp frost had long hardened the crust, through which our feet no longer sunk, and frosted our hair, freezing stiff every part of our garments that had been wetted during the snowstorm. Somewhat large and beautiful crystallizations formed upon the ground in tiny flowers and leaf-like form. As we stood upon the crest of Myrdals, the moon broadened upon the now dark, evening sky, shedding a flood of light across the sea towards the black coast of Myrdalssandr, sharpening the outlines of the thousand crags before us, deepening their shadows and spreading its silver light over glacier and snow. The reflection from the ice threw out in bold relief the dark, volca-

ENCAMPMENT AT GEYSER (*taken in* 1871).

nic formations at our feet, the icy peaks of distant mountains, and the broad, shadowy glaciers of Vatna and Skaptar, which, glistening with a supernatural radiance, made us pause and almost hold our breath as we stood and gazed upon the weird beauty of that calm and silent scene.

We descended at a brisk pace, taking hold of each other's hands, and sliding considerable distances upon the smoothly-frozen crusts which now covered the sides of Myrdals. We arrived at camp about 1 A.M., and heartily appreciated our supper (query breakfast); and a sound sleep rewarded us for our day's exertion, though we had been repaid a thousandfold already by that one view from Myrdals Jökull, not only for our day's efforts, but for all the troubles, difficulties, and expense incidental to our journey from England.

August 3rd.—We were all now confident that the horseshoe-shaped valley must be Katlugia, although it was south-east of its position upon the map, and all traces of activity were buried fathoms deep in its icy bosom. We resolved to visit the volcano upon the opposite side of the valley, and to follow up the sand and other volcanic *débris* to the Valley of Katlugia. It was difficult to believe that the little wavy line upon the map represented the Katlugia which has wrought so much desolation, and presents such terrific proportions to those who care to climb and see it as it really is.

The Valley of Katlugia is, in fact, a large lateral crater of the volcano, of which Myrdals and Merker Jökulls are portions. Around the sides were numerous openings, now partially obscured by ice and snow, leaving a series of banks of sand and cliffs of ferruginous and almost stratified felsite round the margin of the valley. I started at 9 A.M. with only my two Icelanders, W—— wishing to explore the crags and precipices round our camp, so as to collect specimens of the variously-coloured obsidian we had previously noticed. The Icelanders declared that they could not, and would not, cross the valley below, so I started down the side of the precipice alone; but before I got half-way across, I saw them following by a different route. The glacier was very badly crevassed; but it looked worse than it really was, owing to the quantity of black sand mingled with the ice. At this point I found the glacier to be 300 feet lower than the plateau upon which we were camped.

The volcano to which we were now making our way was surrounded by beds of sand and *débris*, and many singularly-formed fragments of felsite, some of which resembled the beading of a cornice. The only traces of lava were numerous fragments of a compact species and obsidian, most of which appeared to be more or less scratched by the glacier. On reaching the side of the crater, the inside walls of which were perfectly perpendicular, rising to the height of 200 feet, I found them to be composed of alternate beds of black ash and soft agglomerate: the bottom of the crater was a deep pool of muddy water, of about 100 square yards. The water was of no perceptible taste, though an unmistakably sour smell arose from it, caused by sulphuric acid, and though many small streams ran into it, I could see none running out. This little volcano was breached to the south, and seemed to have sprung out between three hills of hard ferruginous basalt, now deeply covered with ejectments from the volcano. In several places the basalt was blistered, and blisters such as the specimen I brought home, with care, were readily broken out from the rock. I could see no traces of recent activity, nor is there any record of its ever having been in eruption. No visible lava streams have flowed from it, and it appeared, like Katlugia, to have ejected only water, sand, and fragments of various matter. The bottom of the crater was 50 feet below the surface of the surrounding glacier.

Many hummocks of ice and sand occurred in front of the breach, and extended eastward, stretching out, at last, in dark waves of sandy ice. This sand must have been scooped out from the face of the mountain, for there could be no adequate falling down of sandy detritus from the adjacent sides of the crater before-named to account for that immense accumulation of sandy moraine. A series of low hills, nearly buried in sandy ice, led the way up the Valley of Katlugia. In the middle of the valley the ice was bulged up and rifted in all directions; perpendicular cliffs of felsitic rock, in five places, protruded round the sides of the valley; and in the south corner was a rather large pool of water. I collected specimens of these cliffs and several portions of lava from a long, sandy bank, which had risen along the north-east side.

We toiled up the snowy walls on the west side of the valley, passing many large crevasses, cutting seventy steps before we reached the top. We crossed the Jökull to the south amidst a hailstorm, and returned to camp much satisfied with our expedition. W—— had gone on down to the cave at the foot of the mountain, where we had previously arranged to follow. We took a farewell meal between the rough stone walls that had sheltered us so well, and packing up our belongings, bade adieu to Katlugia and Myrdals Jökull, round which the evening clouds were beginning to cluster in no very promising fashion. We found W—— awaiting us at our trysting-place, and passed a very cold night in the cave; for, to my mind, a cave is the most unpleasant place to camp in: its cold gravelike feeling is more suggestive of rheumatism than a comfortable night's lodging, and unless the weather is very bad I always prefer the open air.

August 4th.—By midday we arrived at Hethi, and at once began preparations for our start on the morrow to Vatna Jökull, agreeing to take with us Sigurd, who had behaved so bravely and well during our short trip upon Myrdals.

We were getting very short of money, for the expenses, now falling upon two instead of four, were more than we had calculated upon. The priest, therefore, very kindly allowed the sum we owed him to stand over until we could obtain additional resources from Reykjavick: in the meantime, we proceeded to Vatna Jökull. We divided half of everything that belonged to the expedition, leaving half of the things with the tent for our quondam travelling companions, and packed up the remaining half for ourselves.

August 5th.—We got under weigh about 11 A.M. It was a lovely day. We were much tormented with numerous flies of the mosquito tribe, which hovered in swarms around our own and our horses' heads throughout the valley of Myrdals. Myrdals means "fly valleys." The good parson from Hethi accompanied us.

The road to Hoffdabrekka was through a series of

gulches, worn by the streams which find their way down from the Jökull to the sea; until, ascending the high ground, we found ourselves at Hoffdabrekka. The church and farm of Hoffdabrekka is perched upon a high bluff overlooking the huge waste of Myrdals Jökull and the lava fields of Skaptar. The River Mulakuis runs at the foot of the bluff, and is a glacial river, having its rise in Myrdals Jökull. It is broad, somewhat deep, and very rapid, and brings down sand in great quantities to the sea. From Hoffdabrekka there is a view of the whole tract of land lying between it and Orefa Jökull. The day was clear, and the waves which broke upon the flat sandy shore could be plainly seen through the telescope. Upon this shore had been cast every plank of which the farm and church of Hoffdabrekka were built. The south coast of Iceland is bountifully supplied with timber from the driftwood, which the gulf stream brings up from America, and which the fierce storms of winter and summer cast upon the shore. For this wonderful provision of nature for treeless Iceland, the natives cannot be too thankful. Every plank one meets with upon the south coast bears evident traces of its long voyage from a more favoured country. Almost every piece of timber is perforated by the *Teredo navalis*, and the logs which were the homes of those molusc navigators now form the dwellings of the grateful Icelanders.

We crossed the River Mulakuis, and here took leave of our friend the clergyman of Hethi, and continued our journey in company with the postman, who was going to Presbakki, where we expected some letters from England; for we were not allowed to take them from the post-bag before they reached the place to which they were consigned. We passed to the east of Hjörleifshofthi, which rises like an island from the plain, in the same manner as Petersey, the hill I described opposite to Fell. From this point we had a magnificent view of Myrdals Jökull and the black sandy sea of Myrdalssandr, leading up almost into the crater of Katlugia. We noticed a rather remarkable feature in the scenery: many of the summits of the surrounding mountains rose bleak, black, and bare to an altitude far beyond the snowy coating upon Myrdals Jökull. The fact is, the accumulated snowfall upon these heights is too insignificant to resist the power and heat of the summer sun; while the immense accumulation upon Myrdals Jökull at the same level, lying as it often does upon a névé or glacier, is continually refrigerated, withstands the solar attack which reduces the snow upon the peaks of the neighbouring mountains to water. The mirage upon these plains is very noticeable. Sheets of water and castellated rocks, slightly raised in the atmosphere, appearing to bound the plain, where there is nothing to break the even line of sand that really limits the vision. We discovered that the little dog Bran, from Hethi, was following us; and as our friend the pastor was now out of sight, it became imperative on us to take our little friend along with us. In this part of the island the track is marked out with white posts, and without the aid of such guidance, it would be impossible to cross these sandy wastes in bad weather. A strong breeze began to blow into our faces, raising clouds of sandy particles, which were very trying to the eyes. Having crossed the Eyjara, a river of some width, with a treacherous bed of quicksand, our course lay over an old lava stream, nearly buried in the sand. It appeared to be a lighter and less compact lava than any I had before seen, and had flowed in a southerly direction. Neither of the Icelanders could tell me whence it came. Crossing the River Jökull Vatn, we caught sight of the farm and church of Thykkvibœr, where Mr. J. Milne and I stayed in 1871; and, for the sake of " auld lang syne," I rode up to it, and greeted its occupants, who regaled me with a draught of milk. At the farm of Myra, which we reached at 10.30, we aroused the priest, who shewed us all needful attention. The priests everywhere seemed to recognise my friend the Rev. W—— as a brother, and more than once I found it a great convenience, apart from the personal ability and help of my companion, to have the authority of his cloth for all I did and said. Many a time, when the Icelanders seemed a little doubtful whether they should obey or not, a remark from me that "the priest" said so-and-so, or that he required them to do this or that, produced a greater effect than all the threats of non-payment of wages, or than any expostulation could have done. The priests have an increasing influence and authority in Iceland; for, apart from their position as head of the flock, they are generally the most wealthy inhabitants of the neighbourhood, though poor enough according to our own ideas of wealth.

August 6th.—I had a long " confab" with the priest, as well as my meagre stock of Icelandic words would allow me, as to the recent eruption in Vatna Jökull, as seen by him from Myra. The sun was shining beautifully upon the Jökulls, as, sitting upon a large weather-beaten plank behind the house, we listened to the description of various eruptions from Vatna and Myrdals Jökull. The pastor told us that the reflection, or, as he called it, "the fire," and the great column of smoke, appeared to rise to the north of the two black conical prominences, which were now the last points visible upon the Vatna; they were the Hágaungn-hjnukur of which I shall hereafter speak. Taking out my azimuth, I found the point to bear a little east of Kaldbakr, in a line from Myra: this, with the line I had taken from Reykjavick, which was 64·30 east upon the Icelandic map, makes the direction from Nupstad NNE. In vain we gazed through the telescope for evidences of present activity. Beyond the black summits of the Hágaungn-hjnukur the vision was bounded by a horizon of perpetual snow. The priest having commissioned us to carry the wafers for the Holy Sacrament, which was to be administered at the next church, we left Myra about 11 A.M., and proceeded to cross the Kutha Fljot, a river of considerable size; and now, as the sun was very hot, it was deeper than usual, owing to the melted snows of Vatna and Skaptar Jökulls. It took us three hours to cross it, being obliged to pick our way from one bank to another, and being stopped at many points by deep water that was running too rapidly for our horses to swim across with their loads upon their backs. When the weather is fine, rivers such as this should always be crossed at night or early morning, or serious accidents might occur. We, however, landed on the opposite shore without further damage than a wetting; and having wrung the water out of our clothes, our guide and the postman set off to the *boer* (Icelandic name for farm), a short distance away, which belonged to a farmer whom I had hired as guide at my former visit to the island; while W—— and I stayed behind to lunch. On resuming our march, we safely deposited the box of sacred wafers entrusted to our care at the church of Langholt, and halted for the night at the farm of Vergr, upon the west bank of the River Eldvatn, *i.e.* "fire water." This river flowed down from Skaptar Jökull at the end of the last century. It is not the great River Eldvatn, which runs into the Kutha Fljot, and takes its name from the same cause, but a smaller river, that rises in the lava stream; most likely fed by the waters of the great Eldvatn, which probably find their way through a series of caverns and hollows, and spring out from the little Elvatn, while the main body of the river flows down to swell the waters of the Kutha Fljot. We had taken the precaution to bring a lamb from Hethi, so I at once prepared a stew and some chocolate. There was a plentiful supply of fuel here, and stacks of timber and a saw-pit shewed the thrifty farmer did no small business as a timber merchant. In this place, as in many others, the people expressed a strong desire to purchase W——'s boots, which were a pair of thick shooting boots: they were very importunate upon this matter. What their idea of our finances must have been I cannot tell; but to ask an English clergyman to sell the very boots he had on his feet was rather a joke. Throughout Iceland, as upon the American frontiers, people seem to fancy you would sell anything you possess, if you could only get a profit by the transaction. The river seemed to be the beau-ideal of a trout and salmon river, so W—— accordingly went fishing in its waters, but with little success: we were informed by the farmer that "the trout only came up from the sea at certain seasons of the year."

August 7th. — W—— having found some peculiar ferruginous formations in the bed of the river, though it was a wet day, we made it our first work to examine them. The lava stream here is tossed up in huge waves of scoriaceous lava, in some places grown over with excellent herbage, and in other parts buried in sand. The lava at this point has not crossed the river: the west side is a shelving slope of sandbanks, which have been cut out by various floods, to the depth, in some places, of twenty feet. The receding waters have left these sloping banks of black sand, upon which were patches of oxide of iron formations, like little red rusty fingers and protuberances, all of which were bored through longitudinally, and stood upright in the sand. Upon

HILLS BEHIND GEYSER.

digging out a few specimens, the cause of their occurrence was apparent. The sand that now forms the surface of these plains, no doubt, covered a fertile tract of land; and the water which percolated through it from the Eldvatn, was saturated with iron. The result was that all organic matter that had been covered by the sand soon accumulated a coating of oxide of iron; and these formations were stalks or stems, coated in some instances to a thickness of half an inch. After we had crossed the Eldvatn, on our way to Presbakki, we observed that the lava had itself formed many small cones, which I should say, from the disposition of the lava round them, had during the progressive flow of the molten matter underneath, long after the surface crust had cooled, acted the part of miniature volcanoes, the lava having welled up and formed tiny streams upon their sides.

We had a very wet ride, and having crossed the River Geirlandsá, we found ourselves at Presbakki, where there is both a church and parsonage. This was the destination of our postman; but the priest, who acted as postmaster, had gone to Thingvellir to see the grand doings in honour of the Royal visit to Iceland; so the mail could not be opened until the Sysselman was sent for. He arrived on the following morning, but none of our letters had been forwarded; so our long journey, out of our way, was useless as regarded them, though it brought us into acquaintance with the priest's nephew, Paul Paulsen, who we afterwards found to be an invaluable assistant.

The morning was bright, though there had been heavy rain in the night. We left Presbakki for Nupstad, a distance of 25 miles. Our road lay across a black, sandy plain, which in dry windy weather is intolerable. A scanty herbage and a few patches of wild oats, together with the rain of the previous night, made the ground in good order for travelling; and as we were so near our destination, we did not scruple to make our horses put their best foot foremost. Before us stood the beetling crags which overhang the farm of Nupstad, and farther to the SE. the snow-clad heights of Euriffa, the highest mountain in Iceland, with its glaciers sloping down apparently to the sea. To our left, and north, were the fine basaltic cliffs which skirt the outlying hills of Vatna and Skaptar Jökull, sweeping in graceful curves, and, terrace after terrace, displaying beautiful columnar structures. Numerous caves, some of which have their weird Norse legends, indicated, perhaps, the wash of oceans, long before the eye of man ever rested on the dark crags they penetrate. Mountain streams, now swollen by the previous rain, leaped from the summit, and dispersed themselves in spray long ere they reached the bottom of the black cliffs; collecting again, as if by magic, underneath, rippling along between the lava blocks, and spreading out upon the broad, black, sandy plain. It was difficult to believe it was the same band of foam which we last saw losing itself over a precipice of 200 feet. To our right, and south, beyond the small, black desert and grey lava-fields, was the ocean, glittering in the sun, which now shone down so warmly, that we were glad to ride along in our shirt-sleeves, and many were the hopes expressed that we might have weather like the present for our trip upon the Vatna Jökull. What are those rocks and ridges jutting out into the sea? that cluster of mushroom-shaped objects half way across the plain? Surely they were not there five minutes ago! It is but the mirage which we have noticed ever since we struck the broad flat plains of sand and lava; but at this time the appearances were plainer than usual, perhaps in consequence of the heavy rain which had fallen during the night. These forms are constantly varying, sometimes seeming like rocks, men, cattle, and farms, in places where we are sure that none exist. The nature of the larger images is easily detected, by the tremulous movement characteristic of the phenomenon; but the smaller ones are very deceptive. Here we find the same illusion so familiar upon the prairies of Western America, a weed or rock being so highly magnified and distorted in shape as to appear as a tree or shed, or some other well-known object. After riding several hours, we reached the lava, which has flowed down the valley of the Diupá from the Hágaungn Hjnukur, or Highgone Hills, upon the south of Vatna Jökull: they are the last points visible from the surrounding country. The lava, which has flowed down the bed of the River Diupá in one deep stream, here spreads out upon the plain in a much thinner flood, towards a large salt marsh leading to the sea, where it terminates in a bed of clinker and volcanic *débris*. The lava is fine and cellular, containing minute crystals of feldspar. The River Diupá means "deep river," and is a dangerous fiord, especially when the water is at all high, for its bed is full of deep holes in the lava, which are very trying to the horses, and may give the careless rider a wet skin.

We reached Nupstad about 4 P.M., and were welcomed by Ayolver the farmer, who was expecting us, and remembered my former visit to his farm in 1871. During the interval which had elapsed, his wife had died, and he had just married again; a fact which occasioned a bountiful supply of provender, and elicited from us complimentary speeches befitting the event.

After seeing to our horses, our first inquiry was whether we could hire men for our expedition; but we were dismayed by the reply that not a man could be spared, for they were already behindhand with their hay harvest, in consequence of the marriage festivities; and every man, woman, and child had now to work their hardest to make up for lost time. Moreover, the farmer added that he doubted if we could get men from any of the neighbouring farms. This was, indeed, "a damper." At this season of the year, the hay is the all-important question; for, unless the Icelander makes hay during the few days that the sun *does* shine in the last two months of summer, he gets no other chance, and it is a poor prospect for his unfortunate cattle through the long dreary months of winter.

Affairs being thus desperate, Paul Paulsen, who had his heart thoroughly in the work, after snatching a hasty meal—and although he had ridden from Presbakki—at once took a fresh horse to scour the country for men to accompany us. We were lodged in a little church, which was used as a store-house, there being no pastor to hold service in it. The good people at Nupstad did all that lay in their power to accommodate us; and after the rough travel we had experienced we quite relished the better food, cleanliness and comfort of Nupstad, for though an Icelandic house cannot come up to our idea of cleanliness exactly, these people were perhaps as clean as it was possible to be under their circumstances. My companion, W———, was quite delighted with the view of the castellated rocks behind the "boer," which I had before described to him. These rocks run to the height of about 300 feet, and appear to grow more and more like battlements; even since my last visit, in 1871, the basalt has fallen away considerably, cleaving off in the regular angular masses peculiar to this formation, so much resembling the ruined works of man. In the afternoon we took a walk to the Sola River, which flows down from the Vatna. The waters from the melted snow collect in the little lake of Grimspotn, some 3,000 feet above the sea level, from whence the river flows down a deep cañon to the sea.

On our way we passed a huge rock, which stands to the east of the farm. It is several hundred feet high, and is cleft in several places, from the top nearly to the bottom. The face of the rock curves inwardly, and when viewed from some aspects it has the appearance of a church organ, the columnar basalt representing the pipes. We stopped to listen to the remarkable echoes which exist here, and which, even more than its form, make it deserve the name we gave it of "Organ Rock." Our shouting scared out a few gulls and ravens, and we continued our ramble to the point where the River Sola first comes into sight. Here we turned to view the basaltic terraces which sweep round and terminate the Bjorns, which hills are here the first step from which the Vatna rises. In many places, especially to the west of Nupstad, the columnar structure is very marked; but the columns are perpendicular, and have none of the fan-like divergence or convergence so remarkably striking in other parts of the island. I saw no traces of dykes in these cliffs, although I searched for them throughout our ramble.

This river has wonderfully altered since I last visited it; instead of being a deep, single stream, rolling with swift and steady current over a shingly bed, it is now shallow and ten times broader, struggling over a bed of loose, black sand, and apparently there is a greater amount of water flowing. The glacier upon the east side of the river has advanced, I should say, half a mile, there being much more sand mingled with the ice and nevé; perhaps the production of some bygone eruption of the Vatna, has been worked down by the glacial action, and has just come to light, after being buried for years in ice and snow.

Although the glacier has advanced, it has lost considerably in height, and is altogether altered in appearance. Before we left the Sola the clouds, which had lain so heavily upon Euriffa all the day, began to roll away, and the summit was plainly discernible, although the remainder of the mountain was obscured. As we returned towards the farm we remarked how lofty the Icelandic mountains looked considering their stated height, but remembered that they generally rise directly from the sea level.

Sunday, August 9th, was spent in quiet. Paul returned, and with much difficulty had succeeded in obtaining two recruits for the expedition; and then, without delay, we began to arrange the supplies, and direct the manufacture of a hand-sleigh and a pair of snow-shoes.

The clouds had settled upon the hills, and the wind had shifted to the east. Towards noon it began to rain. What a difference the weather makes in Iceland, where one's pleasure entirely depends upon open-air enjoyment! I can conceive of no place more utterly wretched in wet weather, or more truly enjoyable in fine.

August 10th was spent in arranging my supplies and provisions for the ascent of Vatna. This consisted of butter, stockfish, biscuit, Liebig's Extract of Meat, and a kind of pemmican I prepared for the purpose, sugar and whiskey; also coffee and soup for use during our first day's march upon the Fjall. I gave to each man a little bottle, to be constantly filled with snow and kept in his bosom; for the want of water is one of the principal difficulties upon these Jökulls. It is impossible with a spirit lamp to melt enough snow for a large party; moreover, it takes twice as much spirit to reduce the snow to water as it does to boil it. On reaching the line of perpetual snow, in addition to the absence of water, one is plagued with an increased thirst, owing to the evaporation from the body. I found the best plan (as it is dangerous to eat snow) was that each man should carry a small flask, wrapped in flannel, in his bosom. Into each flask I from time to time poured in a little whisky, in order to make the snow melt quickly, and render the water more palatable. I also took care that each man should keep his flask filled with snow, and thus secure the advantage of having a few mouthfuls of liquid always at hand.

On Tuesday, *August* 11*th*, the weather cleared, and everyone was in good spirits. W——, myself, the farmer, Paul, Biartny and John, my two fresh men, sat down to a substantial meal in the new room which the farmer had just added to his house. The repast consisted of pickled ox-head, a remnant of the marriage feast, and doubtless kept for our entertainment. I could not help remarking how much more fitting such a start was for men about to undertake a rough trip, than is often the case in other countries from an hotel, where waiters are buzzing about, and people getting in the way. Here everything was deliberate, the food simple, clean, and wholesome, and everyone meant business, as we all stood up to drink success to the expedition in some Scotch whiskey. We then mounted our horses, and crossing the River Diupá we turned to the north, up the valley through which that river flows. It is down this valley that the lava stream I have before mentioned descended from the Highgone Hills : it appears to have advanced at a very rapid rate, descending about 2,500 feet in eight miles; it entirely takes up the former bed of the river. The sides of the lava present a remarkable instance of subsidence, abounding in lateral cracks and rifts throughout its course, full of wonderful, basaltic columns; down these rifts the torrent pours in magnificent waterfalls and foaming rapids. About half-way up the valley, upon the right, a black, basaltic cliff, several hundred feet in height, has been cleft to its centre by some violent convulsion of nature, forming a dark chasm, whose gloomy depth the eye can scarcely penetrate. Down this cleft one-half of the Diupá is precipitated in a roaring mass of foam upon the lava bed more than a hundred feet beneath. The other arm of the Diupá takes its rise from an icy cavern in the glacier several miles to the east, towards Grœnafjall. In two bounds, it sweeps clean down a slope of ice to the valley, and, fed by various glacial streams, it rushes along, till, striking the lava-field, it spreads in sheets of foam; then joining the other arm which has found its way from the snows of the Bjorns, it pours through the chasms in the lava forming the deep river (so well deserving its name), in whose turbid waters no fish can live.

We stopped to lunch at mid-day, and on resuming our journey we disturbed several flocks of ptarmigan, which were feeding upon the little black craig berries, here very numerous. We soon ascended the hills to the left, for it was no longer possible to get the horses over the lava; and now, being upon higher ground, we beheld Vatna Jökull spread out before us—one vast white expanse, terminating in a rough glacier, coated with nevé and black sandy moraine. The two Highgone Hills were now to the NE.; the first about four miles from the edge of the glacier, and the other some five miles farther to the NE. They are black cones penetrating the Jökull; but I could only judge of their nature through the telescope, having no time to give them further inspection.

Our way now lay over a series of quicksands, the horses sinking deeply into the unstable soil at every step, and sometimes entirely falling. On our descent we again found ourselves upon the lava, which here is buried very deeply in light volcanic dust, and appears much thinner than it is lower down. We reached the edge of the glacier about six P.M., being now NNE. of Kalfafell. At this point the glacier had brought down great quantities of obsidian and volcanic *débris*, some of which was apparently identical with specimens I afterwards found upon the Vatna, and also corresponded with others found by Mr. John Milne and myself near Grœnafjall, further to the east, in 1871.

Night was fast approaching, and there was no grass for the horses; so here we parted with W——, the farmer, and his servant. They wished us "God speed;" and I instructed my remaining companions in the art of British cheering: for the first time, I dare say, Vatna Jökull rung with a good round "Hurrah!"

We had brought with us a large tent-cloth of thick canvas, and I had made a large bag of mackintosh sheeting and rugs to sleep in, open at both ends. This, with two blankets, enabled us pretty well to defy the cold. We soon constructed the walls of our tent with the stones we found close at hand, and roofing it with our canvas, we speedily secured a very comfortable shelter. The lamp was soon alight and the soup boiling, and by sundown all was quiet. If anyone could have peeped into our habitation they would have seen only two heads poking out at each end of the bag, and a few wreaths of tobacco-smoke curling gracefully up to the roof of our extemporized abode, finding exit through its various holes and chinks. As I knocked the tobacco ashes from my pipe, I could not refrain from pulling aside the mackintosh coat, which was suspended by way of door, to have a look at the chances for good weather on the morrow. The little glacial stream by which we were camped, owing to the increased cold, was now nearly dry; a cool frosty air stung one's nose, and brought the water to one's eyes; a beautiful moon was rising, making the broad white Jökull glisten with a pearly lustre; the dark waves of the lava stream looked more gloomy and forbidding than ever; the black crags of the Bjorns frowned upon the dark shadows they cast; and the lonely Highgone Hills, away upon the snow, seemed silently and sorrowfully to regard the frozen desolation with which they were surrounded.

We were astir by dawn, and ate the last *warm* meal we were to taste for some time. We then separated from our belongings—the tent-cloth, rope, shovel, sleeping-bag, rugs, instruments, poles, whiskey, and provisions for a fortnight, with the little Union Jack destined to adorn the summit of the Jökull; and the sun, as he rose, was the only witness of the "cache" we made of the remainder of our things. We now commenced the ascent, carrying everything upon our backs, for it was impossible to think of hauling the sleigh over the rough surface of the glacier at this point; for the sand which the ice contained, even if the glacier had been smooth, would have soon worn the runners of a sleigh through by the friction. I had hoped that the surface of the glacier would become clean and smooth after a mile or so, as the part Mr. J. Milne and I had traversed near Grœnafjall in 1871; but I was doomed to disappointment. After an hour's hard work of climbing with our heavy loads over the uneven surface, and dragging the unwieldy sleigh and the snow-shoes (which latter, although of no weight, were the most cumbersome part of our load), we were still surrounded by difficult and bewildering aiguilles, and hummocks of sand and ice, which seemed to increase around us. These obstructions rise to a greater height where the largest quantity of sand occurs, and are caused, as all Alpine travellers know, by the sand protecting the ice of which they are formed from the rays of the sun; while the intervening hollows, originally perhaps mere

VIEW OF RIVER OXERA.

inequalities in the ice, are washed clear of the sand which is constantly working to the top, and so melted to their present depth below the surrounding points.

But, to return:—We paused beneath an aiguille higher than the rest; and as it was evident we all bore heavier burdens than it was possible to carry over ground of this nature with anything like the necessary progress, and as there seemed no probability of our being able to use the sleigh for many a mile, I came to the conclusion that it was better to reduce our loads before we tired ourselves out, by attempting to carry so much over such trying ground. We all agreed that the sheet of canvas, sleeping, and climbing tackle, with instruments and provisions for a week were all that four men could make forced marches with upon a Jökull.

We accordingly abandoned the remainder of our gear; but I carefully took bearings of the spot, and left a pole upon the top of the aiguille under which we had rested, to mark the place. I told my men that we must now travel twice as fast as we had intended to do, and promised them ten dollars each, in addition to their pay, if they reached the point of recent activity in the Vatna, or crossed the Jökull.

I made the things into two large packs of about 70lbs. each, so that two men could carry and two could rest, which is always the best way where speed is the chief object; and serving out a dram all round, I carefully took our direction NNE. once more, and we proceeded at a much-improved pace. There are but few crevasses in this part of the glacier; this is doubtless owing to the small angle at which it slopes. As we stopped to change burdens, for Biartny and John carried first, there was a great rumbling and gurgling in the glacier, which is often the case during the day, owing to the escape of air or water liberated by thawing. I feared my men, who had never before set foot upon a glacier, would be scared; but no such thing! Biartny merely remarked, "How the Jökull is talking!" and John tersely replied, "He speaks well!" The men who were not carrying dragged the sleigh and snow-shoes; but the former became so totally unmanageable amidst the rough nevé and hummocks, that we were obliged to abandon it, as we could improvise an excellent sleigh out of the snow-shoes. We left it three miles NNW. of the first of the Highgone Hills; so if it should ever be found, and the finder will carefully note the position, the rate at which these glaciers move may be approximated. One thing is certain as regards this glacier—it *is* advancing, and possibly ebbs and flows in common with many others of the Icelandic Jökulls. This ebbing and flowing, of course, depends upon the ratio the increment of frozen accumulation bears to the temperature throughout the year. Paul remarked that the Jökull at this point had advanced some 200 yards since he had seen the glacier two years ago from the adjacent Fjall. We noticed some large birds that seemed to be making right across the Vatna Jökull, travelling in the direction we were going. They were much too high for us to make out what species they belonged to, but the very fact of their having such a long dreary flight before them over the snowy wastes which we were about to penetrate made us regard them almost in the light of *compagnons de voyage*, and we could not but envy their easy flight.

The sun was now very hot, and the coagulated snow, which covered the glacier upon which we were walking, became very difficult, and we often broke through into pools of water; so before long I called a halt, having made about seven miles in a straight line NNE.; but as the nature of the ground had compelled us to make several detours, we had covered a considerably greater distance, at the rate of about a mile and a half per hour. We rigged up a shelter from the sun with our poles and canvas, and, after changing our foot-gear, lunched and slept, till the glacier was in better order for travelling. We started again about 6 P.M. It was now much easier going, and the surface of the snow was freezing: the wind NNE. After three hours we were able to pack our things upon the snow-shoes, which we joined together at the toes, leaving the ends to spread out and form a sort of sleigh: it was very light, and travelled easily. We had left the glacier behind us, and for a long while had been travelling over rough nevé, which now developed into pure snow, consolidated by frost, having a crust upon the surface which was beginning to bear us. This mode of progression was much better than carrying the load upon our backs, as the Icelanders said, "*Miklu betra ath draga en bera*," "Much better to drag than to bear," an example of the great affinity between our own language and the Icelandic. The ascent began to be more steep; before it had been scarcely perceptible.

There was now a glorious sunset. The desolate fields of Skaptar and the black summit of Blengre lay beneath us. On the SE. we were fast losing sight of Euriffa, all the more rapidly owing to the elevated nature of the Jökull to the east; but the last view of it can never be forgotten. Its snowy sides reflected an unearthly glow. The sky was perfect, scarcely a cloud was to be seen, and as the sun set, about 10 P.M., it was surrounded with a band of prismatic light; and, for hours after, fitful bands illuminated the western and northern sky, as is always the case in fine weather at the beginning of autumn.

The moon had risen, and a sharp frost had set in, stiffening our hair and beards. Just after nightfall is the clearest time upon the mountains in Iceland, and I looked anxiously for this period, in order to observe whether we could see any traces of smoke to the north. To those who have never looked for smoke in the distance, it may seem easy to distinguish between smoke and cloud; but it is a most difficult task. Again and again I could have said I saw columns of smoke rising, but the appearances soon proved to be only the light clouds of evening.

In this fashion we travelled on till midnight, and then we dug a square hole in the snow and roofed it with our canvas, heaping snow upon the edges to keep out draught. The two ends were fastened up with mackintosh coats, thus as it were having a housetop to cover the hole. We changed our shoes and stockings, hung them upon the ridge-pole, and supped, sitting inside the bag, for it was bitterly cold now we were no longer moving. I put out my thermometer, and found our height to be 4,000 feet above the sea level.

Indescribably beautiful was that moonlight night upon the snow; everything was seen in a strange blue radiance, like that of a Bengal light; no sound or motion—a death-like calm. Crawling back into the warm bag, I finished my pipe, with my nose tucked under the rug. I made every man fill his flask with snow before he laid down, in order that he might have some water in the morning; and thus we snatched three hours' rest.

In the morning my thermometer registered twenty degrees of frost, and our shoes and socks were frozen hard as a board; we had therefore to sit upon our foot-gear, while we breakfasted, before we could reduce them sufficiently to put them on.

It was a glorious morning again, and the sharp frost had frozen everything dry. The snow no longer clung to our shoes, and the sleigh travelled easily over the firmly-frozen crust. After a couple of hours dragging, we sighted a peculiarly-shaped mountain, about ten miles to the NE. The summit was shaped like the end of a house, though at first sight it appeared like a black pyramid. The top was several hundred feet above the level of the surrounding snow; we named it "Vatna Jökull's Housie" —the House of Vatna Jökull.

Further on, to the north, and about two points off our course, lay a black-looking cone, and I made a detour in order to inspect it. It proved to be what I supposed. Cliffs of obsidian rose to the height of 150 feet, varying from a purely vitreous black obsidian to a grey stony variety. They enclosed a small crater breeched towards the NW., while they were surrounded from NE. to SW. by a gulf about forty feet in depth, filled with water, and frozen over, probably an ancient crater, in the centre of which the smaller one had been formed. The cliffs appeared to be constructed by the welling out of lava, rather than from any violent eruption, and when first ejected perhaps displaced an immense amount of frozen material. The surface of the rocks was very brittle, and great quantities of fragments had been split away by the action of the frost. The summit was principally black obsidian, numerous fragments of which lined the sides of the cliffs. This overlaid a more flinty variety, which passed into banded compact laminæ of semi-obsidian, almost a perlite, at times containing large vesicles, which ran into one another; this again developed into a kind of grey stony obsidian. All these changes were apparently brought about by the different stages of cooling through which the lava passed, and the attending circumstances.

We were now 4,500 feet above the sea level. I named the mountain Mount Paul, after Paulsen, who had been so energetic in procuring me men, and without whose aid I should have been sadly at a loss. We enjoyed a good draught of the water, which filled the outside depression, and, watering the whiskey, set off up a steeper ascent due north, in order to allow for our deviation to the east. The great difficulty in acquiring anything like a knowledge of the geology of Vatna Jökull is the depth at which the rocks are buried beneath the snow, and it is only in cases like that just mentioned, or where there may be considerable heat, that it would be possible to gather geological information. At the distance of about seven miles NNW. was apparently a similar crater, but it was more deeply imbedded in the snow. Upon the western horizon were twenty or thirty small black objects, but even through my glass I failed to detect whether they were clouds or black prominences. We journeyed on till we reached the height of 5,750 feet. The sun was very hot, and travelling became exceedingly difficult. The thermometer in the sun rose to 70°, and as we had travelled about ten miles, with a detour of two, to examine Mount Paul, I called a halt, and proceeded to make a contrivance for melting snow. I scooped a hole in the snow, and lined it with a mackintosh coat. I then raised slanting banks of snow round the hole, which I covered in a similar manner, and strewed the whole with snow, leaving a good shovelfull in the bottom of the hole. My companions had meanwhile raised a slant to protect us from the sun.

I ordered all wet socks and shoes to be changed and hung out to dry; for unless great care is taken in this matter, there is soon not a dry change in camp. The men now slept, and I proceeded to post up my diary and take observations.

To the east lay a conical mountain, perhaps a continuation of Vatna Jökull's Housie—distance, about five miles. I could see the black summits of Blengre and the Bjorns, but we had long lost sight of Euriffa. The Bjorns I knew to be SSW. and Blengre SW. Upon taking out my azimuth, great was my dismay at finding the first bearing W. and the latter due north, while my compass performed the most eccentric evolutions. I shut the instrument up in disgust. Contemplating the chance of a fog, and cutting out a circle of paper, upon which I marked the known bearings of Blengre and the Bjorns, I proceeded to take some observations, as far as it was practicable to do so, and drew as accurate a map of my route as was possible under the existing circumstances. I determined to say nothing about my compass being at fault, lest my men might not proceed; so, taking refreshment at my reservoir, which was fast filling, I observed the bearings of the slant, changed my socks, and turned in.

We slept for four or five hours, and rising made a good meal, and drank plentifully of the pool of water, which by this time had collected in our reservoir. All our things were dry, and we were in excellent spirits. As we concluded our meal, a strong smell, as of the carbonic oxide from a blast furnace just tapped, pervaded the atmosphere. We all started to our feet and sniffed the breeze that was blowing pretty strongly from the NNE., which perhaps brought down the exhalation from cooling lava-fields in that direction. I was now doubly sure we were upon the right track. At this moment Paul pulled out the little compass I had lent him to observe more closely the direction of the smell. He at once detected the eccentric movement of the instrument, and exclaimed, "The compass is foolish!" Biartney and John at once crowded round to witness the phenomenon, and, as I expected, asked, "What, in case of fog?" I explained (though I must say, not very satisfactorily to myself) that it was only the part of the mountain we were then on that was attracting it, and asked if they were afraid. They laughed and said, "Oh, no; it is all one to us." I carefully noted the direction of the attraction, which was to the west, that which ought to have been west reading north, though the compass would not hold steadily to any one point. The men called the mountain opposite to us Mount Magnet. It was now freezing, and after advancing a short distance, all ascent terminated in a rolling plain of snow. In vain we searched the horizon for traces of smoke, and when clouds deceived us, even when I was certain, after looking through my telescope, the quick glance of my companions would determine the doubt, with the expression, "*Alla skyæ, ekki reykir,*" "All sky, no smoke." We pursued our way for about three hours more, and passed a beautiful snowy peak to the east, a volcanic cone, covered with snow, and the different stages by which it rose from base to summit told of the series of eruptions which had raised the peak to its present elevation above the surrounding snow, probably 500 feet. Twice did the smell I have described come upon us, each time from the same direction. As the sun was setting we had a magnificent view of two white mountains, evidently volcanoes, away to the east—one, a two-coned mountain; and the other, a smaller one, appeared through the telescope to have a large cave in its side, from which was issuing steam or smoke. I should locate them 12 or 15 miles to the east of our track, but having lost sight of Euriffa and Bjorns, I had nothing by which I could take their angular distance.

When the sun set the surface of the snow became very hard under the influence of a severe frost. Towards the middle of the night the sky clouded over, and as we were much fatigued we again camped, as before, in the snow, 5,950 feet above sea level, determining to rise with the light, and make a long stage before the sun was up. We had been for some hours at about the same level, varying perhaps 100 feet. At supper we reviewed the provisions, and found we had but three days' full rations left, for the severe work in the keen air had greatly increased our appetites. Upon examining my thermometers I found that the columns of both maximum and minimum were broken, and no amount of shaking would adjust them. This, unfortunately, prevented my obtaining any more thermometrical readings upon Vatna Jökull. We slept about four hours, and as it was not yet light in the tent, I tried to peep out, but found an accumulation of snow upon the mackintosh which formed the gable end of our housetop. When I succeeded in removing it sufficiently to look out, I found a thick mist, and fine driving snow prevented me from seeing many yards: to my dismay, the wind was SE., the worst wind in Iceland. I slipped out, without disturbing my companion, and took a good look round. The shovel was nearly covered, only a small part of the handle showing; so I stuck it up in our tracks, the blade bearing N. and S. After this I returned to the bag and slept, trusting the wind might change; but I knew it was hoping against hope, for when the wind

WATERFALL AT THINGVELLIR.

once gets into SE. in this country, there is no knowing how long it will remain there: one thing is certain, it will be the worst weather possible, until it changes. When we all roused up from our sleep, the snow was thickly falling; and as Biartney looked out he remarked, in scarcely a cheerful tone, "*Allt thoka og mikil drifa*," "All fog, much fine snow."

We held a council of war over our breakfast. The men were unanimous in their decision to turn back, nor could I (much as I should like to have done so), with anything like an easy conscience, have tried to persuade them to remain where we were or to go on. We had scarcely three days' provision left; the wind was SSE., where it might stay for a fortnight, as I had often known to be the case; it was hopeless to expect fine weather; the fine snow which was falling shewed there was a great deal more to come, for a heavy fall always begins with fine driving snow, and a passing storm with large flakes, and I did not like the prismatic ring round the sun two nights previous; we were two good days' travel from the commencement of the glacier; our compass was useless, and with the present weather we might be a great deal longer trying to find our way down; I therefore determined to return. We made a good breakfast, duly anathematized the weather, and prepared to leave the English flag, at this our furthest point of progress, and which we believed to be the centre of Vatna Jökull, though the highest point must have been the summit of some of the mountains we saw away to the east. I took one of the poles, six feet long, and attached to it our small Union Jack; then forcing the point down into the snow, we raised a mound around it. I fastened to the pole a little bag, well greased, containing a shilling and a penny, with a note saying we four—W. L. Watts, Englishman; Paul Paulsen, Biartney and John, Icelanders—reached this point and planted this flag-post August 13th, 1874; that Nupstad bore SSW. three days' journey; adding a P.S., requesting the finder of the money *not to squander it in any of the adjacent shops.* The bag was well bound round the pole. On this spot we left "Jack" to endure a lonely existence in the middle of Vatna Jökull, with a stanza of "God save the Queen" from me, and the Icelandic National Hymn of "*Eld gamla Isafold*" from my companions, the tunes of which are nearly identical. Sorrowing that circumstances compelled me to retreat for this year, I bade adieu to the flag of England, and sought the little trace that was left of our back tracks. The tent cover and all that had been exposed to the storm was covered with ice, which made our load much heavier, and I feared we should break the canvas when doubling up the roof that had sheltered us. Fortunately, the wind which most generally brings bad weather in Iceland is not a cold one, or life would be imperilled at such an altitude. The newly-fallen snow made sleighing very heavy, and the exertion made the snow which fell upon us melt to such an extent that we were soon (in spite of our waterproofs) very wet; for it is almost impossible to keep out fine driving snow. The wind blew steadily, and we were assisted by our back tracks, which were remarkably distinct considering the amount of snow that had fallen. The wind, when travelling where it is unaffected by valleys or trees, is a good guide; for there are characteristic winds to every country, the feel of which the traveller soon gets acquainted with, and in thick weather, without a compass, such knowledge is invaluable.

It takes a much longer time to obliterate tracks made in a hard crust than might be supposed, especially upon a slight incline, when it is freezing and a wind blowing: the wind seems to blow the snow in and out again: tracks made in soft snow would not last anything like the same time. I have often remarked this in winter upon the plains of North-West America, to which the summit of the Vatna Jökull bears a close resemblance, especially where the prairies are rolling.

We took it in turns, one to find the way, two to pull, and one to hold the sleigh behind and scoop away the snow which from time to time accumulated in front of it. The ice thickened upon us, making the sleigh much heavier and us less comfortable. After a long and hard pull we reached Mount Paul. My watch had long been broken, so I had left it behind, and now not being able to see the sun, it was scarcely possible with this thick darkness and fast falling snow to tell whether it was night or day.

We descended into the crater for shelter, and breaking away the ice which had accumulated about our neck-wraps and hair, we partook of a good meal, and I again examined the curious rocks around me while my companions filled the flasks with water, and "fixed up" preparatory to another start. The next stage brought us to our snow-house of two days back, but we should not have discovered it had we not most fortunately and unexpectedly hit upon our back tracks again within half a mile from this spot. I never felt more thankful for anything than I did to find I should not have to stand about for an hour in my frozen garments, amid such a tempest, while we fixed a shelter. We soon established ourselves, and having changed our socks, went into the bag, discussing our meal; and as we were all wet and cold, I started Icelandic songs, and we spent some time in shouting ourselves hoarse. Making a noise is a very good thing to warm one, especially in a bag like that my nose was buried in, and, solaced by a short pipe, I fell asleep, while the rapidly-increasing darkness shewed that either it was growing late, or we were getting snowed up.

After a good sleep I awoke, with something pressing heavily upon my face; and I found it was the snow, which had so increased in thickness upon our tent, that it was weighing the canvas down upon us, for we were now using rope as a ridge pole, having left the long pole we had before used with the flag. When we looked out, the wind had shifted more to the east, and if we had had a sufficient stock of provisions I should even then have thought of turning back; but, under the circumstances, it was out of the question. Our shoes and socks were frozen hard again, although we had lain upon them, and we had to put them in our bosoms to thaw them out. Biartney was the first to get his on. He crawled out, leaving a hole through which the snow drifted in a most merciless manner. The house was becoming untenantable, and we were soon all outside, steaming as though we had just been dipped in hot water; but our clothes were soon frozen to our backs. We cleared the snow away and dug out our things. The cold was intense, for now the wind had shifted from the south, and when that is the case the temperature falls very low during bad weather upon these Jökulls.

It took a long while before we felt anything like warm, but in due time the exertion of travelling overcame our icy coating, and the wind being colder made the surface of the snow in much better condition than it had been on the previous day, and we made very good progress—moreover, the men were *going home.*

We travelled hard for many hours, keeping the wind upon our left, and taking turns in pulling, as before, and so reached the termination of the snow. We struck the glacier about four miles west of the first of the Highgone Hills. We were soon obliged to have recourse to our former fashion of carrying our things upon our backs, and after a somewhat dangerous walk, owing to the recently-fallen snow, we arrived at the Fjall where we had left our superfluous luggage. Light was on the wane, so we cooked some soup, which was very grateful; and as we were wet through, and by fording the Diupá at this point we could make a short cut over the Bjorns to Nupstad, we determined to proceed, instead of passing the night upon the Fjall. My men well knew the way, for they are at home amongst the rocks, where they seek their sheep, though they had never before set foot upon a Jökull. We left all our things behind, and raced one another over the lava to the Diupá, which we forded, holding one another round the waist to prevent being swept away, for although it was late in the afternoon, and cold weather withal, there was sufficient water still flowing from the glacier to take us up to our waists. We reached Nupstad before darkness set in, and found W—— awaiting us, and our guide from Reykjavick, who had returned with a fresh supply of provisions, &c. They, with the farmer and his family, gave us a hearty welcome.

In reviewing my trip, as to the light it throws upon the nature of the Vatna, I arrive at the conclusion that the eruptions of last year are neither from the south slope, nor from the centre of Vatna Jökull; they are therefore, doubtless, from a volcano like those I have mentioned, many of which, in all probability, penetrate the northern as well as the southern slope; and from cross-bearings I took of the direction of the eruption as seen from various parts of the island, I should place the volcano from which the eruption came upon the northern slope of the Vatna Jökull, in a line south of Modrudalr, in the north of Iceland, not far from the supposed source of the Jökull Sá of the north, and I mean to direct my next effort towards that spot.

K

In order properly to explore Vatna Jökull, it is necessary that the party should consist of not less than eight persons, with two sleighs that will carry from 150 to 200lbs. each, for although that is too much to journey with on a glacier, it can be easily carried on the snow. The allowance of provisions should be $1\frac{1}{2}$lbs. of meat, $\frac{1}{4}$lb. of butter, 1lb. of bread, $\frac{1}{2}$oz. of sugar, and $\frac{1}{4}$ pint of whisky per man per day. All should sleep in a large bag made of thick mackintosh and blanketing; a cork mattress should also be added large enough to floor the house, with a margin of thin oilskin, that might peg into the walls to prevent the back getting wet when leaning against the sides. Two buffalo skins, or a large eider-down quilt, would also be of service; otherwise there should be a spare rug for each man. More important than all, is some good method of melting snow without the use of spirit lamps. A good tent, eight feet by eight, and three feet high, should also be taken. Two stout iron shovels are indispensable. For clothing, nothing is better than strong tweed knickerbockers, worsted drawers, knitted jerseys, and pilot coat, with knitted socks and Indian mocassins. These last are a *sine quâ non*. English boots are out of the question for snow travelling, and the Icelandic shoes, though better than English boots, require tops to be sewn on them.

Snow-shoes for those who can use them are a great assistance.

To sum up, this hitherto untrodden Vatna Jökull is a mountainous tract, surmounted by a rolling plateau, containing numerous volcanoes, one or more of which, upon the north, appear to be in a state of pretty constant activity, while numerous others in all probability are paroxysmal, most likely exhibiting all the phenomena characteristic of (if I may be allowed the term) *bottled up volcanoes*. This tract, together with the Odatha-hraun, and the centre of Iceland with its numerous mountains, is a new volume of Nature, the first leaf of which has only just been cut, but whose secluded fastnesses will amply repay investigation.

August 17th.—It was a great relief, after our recent hard work, when I awoke on Sunday morning and found myself beside my friends in the little church at Nupstad, with the fresh stores from Reykjavick about us; and as the good housewife came in with our coffee, and I called out to Guthminder to cook some ham for our breakfast, I felt the contrast between my present surroundings and those of the two days previously. By no means the least important of the necessaries brought from Reykjavick was an addition to our exchequer, without which we should have been in a very awkward predicament.

After washing in a small mountain stream, which in 1871, as now, I had used as a lavatory, we breakfasted. We strolled through the lava of the Diupá towards the termination of the stream. It ended in a high bank of *débris*, at the foot of which we found several springs of pure cold water, forming a trout stream of some size, which flowed through a salt marsh towards the sea. This, as I have before remarked, is a very common feature in connection with lava streams.

August 18*th*.—We bade adieu to our hospitable Nupstad friends, leaving behind us a few articles in case of a future visit. I should have organized another expedition to Vatna, but my funds would by no means allow of my doing so, for money forms the sinews of travel as well as of war. On returning to Presbakki, we passed Gunnershellir, a cave in the basaltic cliffs. There is a tradition that a man named Gunner, who was an outlaw, with a band of followers, formerly dwelt there. In order to scale the cliff that cut it off from the ground below, it was necessary to procure a ladder, which Paul assured us he could obtain from Presbakki. Presbakki is one of the new-fangled farms, built in the Danish farmhouse style of Reykjavick; they are more commodious, and admit of more ventilation and cleanliness than the old-fashioned Icelandic house, which is built of lava blocks and turf. But they are much colder, and there is often an air of pretension about those who aspire to this new style of building, which is fatal to comfort, and, moreover, one has often to pay in proportion.

I said to the priest of Presbakki that I should like to visit the volcano of Skaptar Jökull, whence the great lava stream of Eldvatn had flowed; and although he asked forty dollars for a man and horse to guide us, we intended going.

Upon counting up our money we found that we could not afford forty dollars, and so I informed the clergyman that we had altered our plans, and would not go to the Skaptar. We asked if we could hire a man and a ladder go to Gunnershellir, not quite a mile distant: for this ten dollars were demanded, so we relinquished the gratification of inspecting the outlaw's retreat, rather than be so fleeced.

Upon asking what we had to pay for our accommodation, we were told that nothing would be asked. but that he left it to us to give what we thought fit. Anywhere this is an unsatisfactory kind of remunetion, and we had no idea of adopting it now, as we had met with the style of thing before, and mostly in the new-fashioned houses. I imagine it is done with the hope that the guest will give more than the host would like to demand. In such cases it is best to give what is the usual and proper charge, viz., eight skillings for each horse, half-a-dollar for each man if the traveller has his own provisions, and one dollar if he has not, always paying in even dollars, as a matter of course. It is a practice with some of the guides to suggest a gift to the church; but as that is equivalent to giving twice as much as the lodging is worth, it is best to avoid doing so, both on your own account and that of travellers who may follow. Travelling in Iceland is no exception to the general rule—it resolves into a matter of pounds, shillings and pence; nor are the Icelanders any exception to other nations in respect of extortion. There is the usual amount of the good and the bad of hospitality and churlishness to be met with, though, perhaps, I should qualify this by saying that upon the whole there is more of hospitality practised here than among many other nations. The good, genuine, old-fashioned Icelander is an honest, hospitable, open-hearted fellow, and is relatively the same as the good old style of Englishmen; but whether nations improve individually in the virtues of goodwill and hospitality from the social advantages of civilization, is a matter which even my few peregrinations have taught me to doubt. The following statistics may help to give an idea of the hospitality which we experienced, going and returning, between

Reykjavick and Vatna Jökull. Out of twenty-six entertainments, I met six instances of great hospitality, six of hospitality well paid for, nine of fair treatment for fair pay, and five instances of churlishness and extortion. Upon taking leave, we were surprised to have a charge made of five dollars for catching and shoeing the horse we intended to have taken to Skaptar; and, upon our objecting, the priest presented us with the little memorandum, saying, in a voice calculated to inspire unlimited respect, "Latine! Latine! Primus ludibris me habuisti eques, duos proxima nocte arressedos duos servos a opere necessaris prohibendi." Whether it was for the imaginary mocking, or the sending his servants to catch two horses, that the extra five dollars were charged, did not appear; but as we had already paid five dollars for accommodation, we only offered three in addition, which the priest would not take, and they were given to Paul, his nephew. "It is an ill wind that blows no one any good," even in Iceland.

We now came to a settlement with Paul, who was of a very different disposition, and would insist upon accompanying us for two days, in token of his regard for us; and as he was perfectly acquainted with the road we were now taking, his assistance was valuable in the extreme. It began to rain heavily, and as our horses were getting rather wayworn, we stopped at Arnardrangr for the night, Paul proceeding to some friends at another farm. The next day Paul met us a mile or two from our last halting-place, and pressed us to accept two bottles of schnaps as a parting gift. We here parted with him, expressing mutually our wishes that we might travel together again on some future occasion.

Further on we perceived a swan's skin hanging outside a little "boer." We purchased it for a dollar, and took the "bonder" (farmer) as guide to shew us the ford across the River Eldvatn. On the bank of the river we stopped to examine the lava stream upon the east side. The lava had cooled in large waves, now nearly covered with sand, and in many places covered over with excellent herbage.

We selected two specimens, one from the bottom, the other from the top of the stream; and then set out for Myra, crossing the Marga Fljot, in which there was now but little water, it being 8 P.M. We arrived at Myra in an hour. It rained so heavily that we consulted our comfort by remaining at Myra, as there was plenty of time to get back to the steamer which was to convey us to Scotland. A lovely morning followed, with a slight frost. We could see the surrounding Jökulls and mountains distinctly; all of

CHURCH AND FARMHOUSE AT THINGVELLIR.

them were white with recently-fallen snow. I doubt if there be any view of distant mountains that can surpass that from Myra: the towering heights of Orefa to the east, the broad slopes of Vatna and Skaptar, with the outlying ranges of black volcanic hills towards the north, Myrdals, Godalands, and Merker Jökulls to the west and north-west; while, upon a sunny morning, can be seen the glittering outlines of the distant ocean, extending from east to west. The rain of the previous day had laid the terrible sand upon Myrdals Sandr, or we could not have crossed it with the wind that was now blowing, especially riding with it directly in our teeth, as we were now doing. When we were about half way to Hoffdebrekka, we met Mr. Thorgrimmer and his equipage upon a journey of postal inspection. He gave us an account of the grand doings in honour of the King of Denmark's visit to the island.

There was but little water in the Mulakuis, and we found a ford across it without difficulty. Our horses seemed now to know their way and to improve their pace as we progressed towards Hethi. We arrived there at 8 P.M., and found the good people still busy with their hay harvest; but our appearance was the signal for them to throw down their implements and come and welcome us, with their usual freedom and hospitality. The next day we took a ramble amongst the hills towards Myrdals Jökull, with many of which I was pretty well acquainted. It was a lovely day, in fact the first really fine day I had had for the Hethi Hills. The material of their construction is soft agglomerate, strewn as usual with a heterogeneous accumulation of fragments, slabs, and blocks of stone, probably brought down, in many instances, by the glaciers. I broke a specimen from a rock, coated as it were with jaspery clay, which I had never seen occurring in such large masses before. We also found a little fragment of lava, shaped exactly like many of the silicifications of Geyser. We reached the height of 2,500 feet, whence we obtained a grand view of the Jökull behind us. From the highest point we saw a steamer out at sea; and after resting for a few minutes at a cave, we returned to Hethi. Small caves are very numerous amongst these hills, and their occurrence for a long time puzzled me; but on many occasions I noticed several in the process of formation. I found that where large slabs of basalt fell out of the agglomerate, a large hollow was universally formed. This became rapidly enlarged by the sweeping in and out of the wind, and in some instances by the wash of small streams. I observed that the hollows having been once formed, when the wind blew from a certain direction it swept in and out of the cavities, always accompanied in its exit by numerous particles from the interior.

I have often seen stems and grass blown in and out of these caves, always accompanied by more or less sand. This scooping influence, to which the soft and friable sides and floor must gradually succumb, seems to account for the numerous cavities which penetrate the hills of Hethi. During our progress home, we crossed the bed of a stream which had cut through the hillside to a considerable depth. Here we found a great number of ashes and volcanic bombs. Upon the adjacent hills were two remarkable masses of rock, which when struck with a hammer sounded perfectly hollow. They were of highly ferruginous lava, and, strange to say, those least metallic gave the most sonorous note. We left Hethi at mid-day, calling at the " boer," Icelandic farm, of Sigurd. He volunteered to shew us the way over the Jökull Sá, which we crossed at 7 P.M. There being but little water flowing, Sigurd took leave of us when within sight of Scogar: he expressed a great desire to be my guide upon my next visit.

We passed the night at Scogar, and the next day left for Holt, having spent the morning in examining the falls of Scogar Foss. A little way past the farm of Steiner we saw a large eagle, sitting upon a rock not many yards from our track. We called a halt, and, unstrapping the gun, loaded it; but during the process the eagle flew away. W—— shot a duck, and I prospected for another over the marshy plain which lay between us and Holt, while my companions rode on, as it was growing late, purposing to catch them up when I had finished my hunt. I sighted a flock of ducks upon a pool, and cautiously made my way towards them; they, however, saw me and took flight; so I urged on my horse to get a little closer shot, but, alas! he trod upon a treacherous bog, shot me over his head, and, upon picking myself up, all that was visible of my poor horse was his head. He struggled bravely, but his efforts were of no avail, and seeing no time was to be lost, I caught hold of his head, and managed to get his fore-feet upon the edge of the pool that he had now formed around him; and finding that single-handed I could do nothing, I left my coat, gun, and case of instruments behind, to let my horse see I intended coming back, and started for the nearest "boer," which fortunately was not more than a mile away, to obtain assistance. I explained my position to the bonder, and told him to fetch a horse and a rope, while I returned on foot to my poor animal. The bonder was there as soon as I was; and although night was coming on, and it was beginning to rain, I was obliged to strip off my clothes, in order to get the rope in position underneath the horse, for, apart from the impossibility of moving about with one's clothes on in the quagmire, the idea of having everything saturated with the foul ooze was hardly pleasant. Being reduced to my buff, I was about to step into the bog, when a female figure appeared, which caused me to take to the mire more readily than I should otherwise have done; and I was rather dismayed when I heard the bonder calling at the top of his voice, " Margaret! Margaret! fara hedna." Margaret did indeed "fara hedna," and a pretty position I was in. The clouds of evening were creeping down the overhanging hills, a gentle drizzle had set in, my horse and I were stuck fast in a bog up to our necks, my clothes were several yards away from me. Margaret had responded to the call for help, and stood there, perceiving no impropriety in the scene. Her one object was to render assistance to the needy, and I could see that the help of her sturdy arm was an absolute necessity if my poor horse was to be saved; but I must draw a veil over this awkward predicament and how I managed to extricate myself from it. An hour's work, and the efficient furtherance of the bonder and Margaret, and my horse was free. The mud was scraped from me with my whip-handle, and I washed in a stream close by. Margaret and the man received a dollar each, and I hastened on to Holt, where the joke of my adventure was fully appreciated.

From Holt we retraced the way we had previously come. At Bretherbolstad we again received every attention, indeed it was at this stage of our progress we began to feel the agreeable consciousness of relapsing into civilization. The next day we left our good friends and proceeded on our homeward journey, stopping by the way at Storrevellir, and putting up for the night at a farm not far from the River Thorsà. We were detained by bad weather nearly the whole of the following day on the eastern bank of the river, but crossed over to Thorsà-holt for the night, as we were in no hurry to reach Reykjavick, having plenty of time on hand. At this place was a natural vapour-bath, much resorted to by the inhabitants. A great volume of sulphurous steam issued from the ground, which was housed over with a hut of lava blocks and turf: a chamber also adjoined for persons undergoing the operation to cool in. This bath is much used by people suffering from the cutaneous diseases so prevalent in the island.

At this point, as I have before remarked, a lava stream from Hecla has crossed the River Thorsà. We proceeded at mid-day to Hraungerthi, where we passed the night in a church, being very suspiciously regarded by the priest, who perhaps, in consequence of our travel-stained appearance, thought we were hardly up to the mark of usual English travellers. He seemed, however, to think that should make no difference in the price of our accommodation.

Our next day's travel was across a marshy flat, towards the river Hvitá. Upon applying at the farm where the ferryman resides, we were informed that he was cutting grass, more than a mile away, upon the marsh we had just traversed. He was quickly summoned by a rather novel expedient. The young lady of the house divested herself of a black homespun petticoat of large dimensions, and, attaching it to a pole, planted it in the turf roof of the house. This soon had the desired effect, for within a quarter-of-an-hour a horse's hoofs were heard splashing the mud in front of the little "boer." An Icelander never walks if he can ride, and in this instance the bonder, as usual, had taken his horse with him, which accounted for his speedy appearance.

Some ancient (?) Icelandic silver jewellery was here exhibited, but we had already purchased similar specimens at other farms, further from the beaten track of tourists. A great deal that was here shewn us smacked strongly of "Brummagem," and was much more expensive than that we had previously acquired.

Having crossed the River Hvitá, we continued our journey to Reykir, stopping by the way to examine some remarkable dykes upon the sides of the mountain Ingolfsfjall. They appeared in the distance like low walls protruding from the mountain side. We climbed up to them, and found they were composed of flat angular slabs, which were easily separated, all occurring upon one another as regularly as though placed there by human design; the broad sides of the slabs being the divisional planes both above and below. We reached Reykir in the afternoon: it well deserves its name of Reykir, " the smoking." The whole valley is perforated with boiling springs, which fill it with steam, each spring sending its contribution of hot water to the little river Varmá, the steaming waters of which flow down towards the mouth of the Hvitá, where it discharges itself: its designation, "Varmá," is quite suggestive of its temperature. Several hot springs occur in the immediate bed of the stream, and there is a small waterfall opposite the farm and church of Reykir. The farmer informed us that there were both salmon and trout in the river below the fall. Two of the largest of the springs occur in the side of the hills to the NE. of the farm. They, like the springs of Laugerdalr, are intermittent; unlike them, however, they deposit a sinter, with which the ground in the neighbourhood of Reykir is strewn.

August 28th.—We had lodged in the church, our horses had fed upon the hill-side, and all we had obtained from the farm was some milk; we were therefore much surprised by the farmer demanding a sum of fifteen dollars for our accommodation. This was outrageous, as many of the charges at the most frequented stopping-places are. When we had made everything ready to start, I called to the farmer and again demanded how much he wanted. He repeated the previous charge, so taking from the bag three dollars, which were ample payment, I said, "I see many foolish Englishmen have been here, and you think all Englishmen are foolish, but they are not; here are three dollars—if you will not have them, never mind, I will keep them." Seeing we were determined, he took them and thanked me. We then proceeded to Herdisuvick, over a lava-field; but the inequalities of our path led us into several difficulties. This place was like a little oasis in a wilderness of lava. We were most hospitably received by the bonder and his family. The surroundings of the farm were greatly improved by the useful and valuable articles the sea had brought almost to its door. For our breakfast they prepared a great treat—blauberries and milk: as we had not tasted fresh fruit for three months, this dish was doubly acceptable. I think, perhaps, one of the articles missed more than anything else during a long trip in these latitudes is fresh fruit; and I am sure that nothing is more conducive to the health and strength of a party than preserved fruit, or, better still, tinned fruit, if it can be managed. We purchased some blue fox-skins; but as it was summer they were not in prime condition.

August 29*th*.—We left our hospitable entertainer's roof at 10 A.M., and made our way towards Krisuvick, accompanied by the farmer, who conducted us over the lava for several miles, and upon leaving us would take no remuneration. The lava in this part appears to have poured down from the higher ground in a viscous flood, bearing upon its surface a stupendous accumulation of scoriaceous matter, piling it up in huge walls and mounds at all points where it had descended from the hills above. Upon reaching the land beneath it appears to have spread out evenly, and with a flow like that of a deep and swift running river, swirling and eddying in its course, filling up depressions and forming thousands of those rope-like formations so peculiar to this species of lava; in some places it had even stretched away to sea, where a foaming line of breakers marks its course, and betrays the existence of the terrible reefs that gird this portion of the southern shore of Iceland.

Half-way between Herdisuvick and Reykjavick are one small and two large mounds of lava-blocks, and our guide stopped here to relate to us the legend concerning them. "This," said he (pointing to the cairns which were close together), "is the mound of Herdis and his son, and this is where Kris lies. A long time ago a man named Kris lived at Krisuvick, and a man named Herdis at Herdisuvick. Kris was a bad man, and hated Herdis. Herdis one day sent his little son to this place to feed sheep; he was met by Kris, who demanded what he was doing on his land; to this the son of Herdis replied, that it was his father's land. This enraged the wicked Kris so much that he slew the lad. It so happened that Herdis was within sight; he ran to the spot, and immediately a fierce fight commenced. After a long combat, Kris was killed; but not before he had mortally wounded Herdis, who fell dead over the body of his son." Their tombs are these rude cairns of lava, which now bound the estates of Krisuvick and Herdisuvick, commemorating upon that stormy coast a deed of cruelty, paternal love, and valour. Upon rounding a bend in the hill the mountains of Krisuvick, with their solfataras, came in to view, from whence a cloud of steam was rising, and crossing the small stream of mineral waters which flows from them, we reached the church and homestead of Krisuvick. As is often the case in a land where there is so little provision for travellers, we lodged in the church.

The hills of Krisuvick, so far as I have seen, are a series of ancient volcanoes, composed for the most part of palagonitic agglomerate, considerable areas of which have been converted into a sulphurous mud by the acid gases exhaled from their now slumbering vents. Having snatched a hasty meal, we proceeded to inspect several of the solfataras. They are patches and hollows of bluish white siliceous mud, the greater part of which is at a very high temperature. They are occasioned by the acid vapours which are still rising from the heated lava far below, which decompose the contiguous rocks and deposit their constituent elements either as fresh combinations or in their simple forms, together with the products of the vapours themselves, notably silica, sulphur, gypsum, and sulphate of iron. It is principally to the oxidation of the latter that the sulphurous muds of Krisuvick owe the variety of their shades and colours. The sulphur sublimates upon the surface of the mud, forming a crust from half an inch to a foot or more in thickness, the under surface of which is covered in many places with beautiful crystallizations of sulphur.

These fumaroles frequently alter their position,

VIEW OF A SOLFATARA AT KRISUVICK.

owing to the heated and corroding vapours finding a readier escape in some other direction, where they speedily establish a new fumarole. The ground in the immediate neighbourhood of many of these solfataras gives out a hollow sound when the foot is stamped upon it. This phenomenon is common to many similar localities in other parts of the world, and has been perfectly explained by Mr. Scroope, who attributes the hollow sound to the multiplied echoes arising from the numerous cavities and cells that have been formed by the vapours of the solfatara during their passage beneath the surface of the ground, producing precisely the same effect as one large one would have done. This also explains the phenomenon of the sonorous rocks I mentioned upon the hills near Hethi. There are about eighty or ninety of these fumaroles in the surrounding hills, and probably there were from one to two tons of sulphur upon those we inspected. At the end of one of the fumaroles, a column of vapour was being emitted with regular puffs as from a locomotive, and we proceeded towards it. Guthminder was first, and W—— next: I had stayed behind, to obtain some specimens of the sulphur. Suddenly the treacherous crust gave way under the feet of my friend. Fortunately, he had the presence of mind to throw himself forward, or he might have sunk up to his neck in the boiling mud before we could have rendered him any assistance. Both his legs were severely scalded, but it was well it was no worse. We returned to the church at Krisuvick, and, happily, obtained sufficient oil to dress the burns. In consequence of this unfortunate occurrence, we rested the next day at Krisuvick, and as soon as we were able took the road for Reykjavick, passing over the desolate country which has been so often described. On the way we met Dr. Hjaltalin and the Rev. Martin Hart, who were bound upon a journey of inspection to Krisuvick.

September 1st.—Our wanderings terminated at the capital of Iceland—Reykjavick, where we had the gratification of selling our ponies for about one-sixth of what we had paid for them, solacing ourselves with the knowledge that they had not cost us more for the use of them, indeed not so much, as many other people had been obliged to pay.

APPENDIX.

One of the first things necessary to the advancement of Iceland as a nation is an improvement in its means of communication with other European countries, more especially during the summer months. At present, the mail steamer "Diana" is the only steam-vessel engaged in regular intercourse with the island. She makes only eight trips in a year. She is an uncomfortable vessel, in consequence of her desperate rolling propensity, and the accommodation, particularly this year, was both bad and insufficient. Considering that the greater number of the passengers are almost always Englishmen, some little regard might be paid to the English appetite and taste.

The passage-money, including provisions, is £8, or £14 for return by the same trip. This ought to be quite enough to provide decent accommodation. Some system of letters-of-credit ought to be established, for, at present, although there is no bank in Reykjavick, it would be perfectly easy for the authorities, or some of the merchants, to establish a mode of communication with one of our English banks. This year (1874) being the 1000th year since the island was first colonized by the Viking outlaws, from whom the Icelandic race have descended, a nominal freedom has been conferred upon it by Denmark. The one aim and desire of the Icelanders, generally, is that Iceland may become a separate and acknowledged country and nation.

Before this can come to pass, two things are indispensable, viz., capital and the co-operation of other countries. In their present condition, the people are, as a matter of course, thrown upon their own resources. These are fish, wool, sheep, horses, cattle, some mineral wealth, and the money brought to them by travellers visiting the marvellous and interesting natural phenomena which their island contains. To develope these resources, however, capital is needed. To enable them to extend their fisheries, which might without doubt be made one of their most fruitful industries, larger and better boats than those now in use are also needed, for at present the Icelanders carry on the greater part of their fisheries in small open boats, utterly unfit for long trips, or fishing on a large scale. Other countries are not slow to take advantage of this inefficient condition of the Icelandic fishermen. The French and the English both reap an abundant harvest from the prolific waters of this northern sea.

The Icelandic wool is abundant, and fine in quality. Both the number and quality of the sheep, cattle, and horses might be much improved by the importation of fresh breeds, and a plentiful supply of compressed fodder from other countries.

With regard to the mineral wealth of Iceland, it appears to me that hopes have been built upon it that will never be realized. At present, the most valuable mineral production is the Icelandic spar (carbonate of lime) at Eskifiord. It is quite possible that this spar occurs in many other parts of the island. The sulphur of Krisuvick does not, I fear, occur in sufficient quantities to pay; nor could it be worked and transported at such a rate as would enable it to compete successfully in the English markets. Travellers, however, who have visited the neighbourhood of Krabla, in the north of the island, have reported very favourably upon the deposits in that direction, and I have no doubt that sulphur occurs extensively in other places. The great drawback to all these would be the impracticable nature of the land which intervenes between such localities and any point upon the sea-shore where it would be possible to harbour vessels. It is quite likely that borax might be found in some of the inland lakes; and if such were the case, its high commercial value would justify the making of roads, which the workers of sulphur deposits could never afford to do. In many places there are rich iron ores; but all the specimens I have seen have been the Titanic iron, which is of little commercial value. There has been a great deal said about the surturbrand of the north: its value can be but local, although such value would be high. I do not know whether it occurs in workable quantities or not.

One source of hard cash, and by no means a small one, would be the encouragement of tourist visitors during the summer months. Of the sporting facilities of the island I am scarcely qualified to speak; but I know that its lakes, and many of its rivers, abound in fish, and that the shooting is not to be despised.

To the admirer of natural phenomena, Iceland offers exceptional interest, and it is to the pecuniary interest of the inhabitants that these objects be made more generally known, and that fresh features of attraction to the traveller be disclosed from unexplored parts of the country. Every Icelander should therefore take an interest in the result of exploring expeditions, and should consider it a matter of importance to his country that travellers meet with good entertainment and assistance, and that only a just and honest price be demanded for what they require. From my own experience the exceptions to the latter have been few, the rule being a fair and equitable demand. It would be a source of great comfort to the tourist, if the Government were to establish a regular tariff for the entertainment of travellers and the hire of guides.

One of the first things to be done, as soon as the country can afford it, will be to make roads, so that wheeled vehicles can be used for carrying necessaries, instead of the pack-horse, which is now the only means of transport, except in the immediate neighbourhood of Reykjavick, where carts have been introduced. Roads might be made before the public coffers are rich enough to pay for their construction: there might be a levy made upon every district, to construct a length of road proportionate to the number of its inhabitants. There might also be a requisition made, requiring every bonder (farmer) to level, clear, and drain a certain portion of land adjoining his farm, making the tenure of the farm dependent on his so doing. A public Society might be formed for the improvement of the breed of their stock; and Fishing Companies might be originated, assisted by the Government, to buy a better class of vessels and tackle.

One great advantage of Iceland is, that there are few political expenses; so that a small tax upon the whole community could be almost all devoted to these purposes.

The main disadvantage of Iceland is its inclement climate. The only crops that attain any degree of perfection are potatoes and turnips, and these vegetables are scarcely sufficient to act as a national antiscorbutic. Under the present condition there certainly seems much that is unfavourable to development; but in a nation so attached to their country, I believe energy might be roused adequate to the endurance of a century of struggle, which might result in enabling the country not only to support itself, but to restore to this dearly-loved island something of its ancient prestige. If the Icelanders are unequal to this great effort, emigration *en masse* to some more favoured land would be the next best thing to do. Of course, Denmark must be favourable to the carrying out of any definite course of action, or nothing can be done, and nations must be willing to acknowledge the independence of Iceland, and ready to invest their money in enterprises as soon as they can see reasonable security.

Iceland is the northern focus of the line of volcanic action, which extends from Jan Mayen, through Iceland itself, the Feroe Isles, the Western Isles of

Scotland, Great Britain, the Azores, Madeira, Canaries, Cape de Verde Isles, Ascension, and St. Helena, to Tristan d'Acunha, in the latitude of the Cape of Good Hope; thus maintaining, through 120 degrees of latitude, a nearly-meridional direction.

Iceland is remarkable for the extensive scale on which its volcanic activity has been developed, more than twenty of its mountains having been seen in active eruption within the historic period; indeed, no district in Europe or Africa can be compared to it in this respect, the only parallels must be sought on the eastern and western sides of the Pacific Ocean.

The lavas seen during my sojourn in the country were, with few exceptions, basaltic. The following are the principal known volcanoes :—Hecla, which has been in eruption thirteen times since the year 1004: two of its craters are in a state of solfatara, and the others are cold and filled with ice. Katlugia has erupted fifteen times since the year 900, and is now perfectly cold, and its huge baranco crater is filled with a glacier. A volcano near Reikianess has erupted three times; one eruption occurred from Lake Grimwata, and two from Eyjafjalla Jökull, from 1724 to 1730. Mount Krabla was in vehement eruption once; Orefa, twice; Trölladyngia, four times; Thingvellir Hraun, twice; Skaptar Jökull, from which proceeded the most violent of eruptions, and from which flowed the largest known lava stream in the world, once—in 1789, and also a volcano upon the north side of Vatna Jökull, which has never been visited, but which has burst forth on several occasions: from this, I have no doubt, proceed the foul smells which are perceived upon its southern base when a strong NNE. wind blows. From this latter circumstance I should almost surmise that it is in a constant state of slumbering activity, for the emanations from a solfatara would not be likely to travel so great a distance.

From the above statement, it will appear that the volcanoes of Iceland belong to the class known as paroxysmal, the most dangerous and treacherous of the whole family; since, by long periods of tranquillity, continued sometimes through ages, they lure the surrounding inhabitants into a false idea of security, and the character of their terrible neighbour is at length only proclaimed by the sudden outburst, destructive alike to life and property.

The mountains of Iceland are divided into two classes—Jökulls and Fjalls. The Jökulls are those covered with snow and ice; the Fjalls are smaller, rocky eminences.

The immense Jökulls exercise by no means a beneficial influence over the climate, and a long series of cold wet seasons might increase the glaciers to such an alarming extent as would be most disastrous to the country; for the more the glaciers increase, the less likelihood is there of fine seasons at all, and thus they might augment in an inverse ratio, which would soon cover the whole island. Hitherto these glaciers have ebbed and flowed in ratio as the repeated series of seasons have been either wet or dry; but there is no knowing how gravely a prolonged series of wet and cold seasons might affect them. Nor is the important part which Arctic and sub-Arctic glaciers play in the economy of the temperature of our climate duly recognised.

To any one who may determine upon a trip to Iceland, I suggest the following hints as to the necessary equipment, expense, and length of time required:—

He should take two pairs of good tweed trousers; two waistcoats; one stout pilot coat; one tweed coat, full of pockets; a complete outfit of waterproof covering, the best he can purchase, or else a suit of oilskin, which perhaps is better; two pairs of alpine boots; one pair of canvass shoes; two football jerseys; two stout flannel shirts, with elastic at the collar and wrists—no buttons; three pairs of woollen drawers; six pairs of worsted socks; four pocket-handkerchiefs; a woollen muffler for the neck; a large blanket rug and a sleeping bag; two towels; one comb; two small-toothed combs, "real necessaries;" carbolic soap; pocket looking-glass; scissors; house-wife, &c.; a stout double-bladed knife; tweezers; wax; an elastic sock, in case of sprained ancle; cap or hat, according to fancy; and two pairs of blue spectacles, with side protectors.

For provisions, take from England, according to the number of the party, pea-soup, in rolls; extract of beef, in skins; Chall's tablets of soup Julienne; bacon; figs; smoked sausages; biscuits; tea; Fry's cocoa, or chocolate and milk; and whiskey. He can procure in the country, mutton, butter, rye-cake, excellent coffee at the farms, fish, sugar, though not much in some parts, game, and poor schnapps. As conveniences, he should take a tent of no great height, *i. e.*, not more than five feet high; waterproof sheets, a cork mattress, frying-pan, three block-tin pots, and stella lamp for cooking; candles, or a small oil lamp, a geologist's hammer, nails, and gimlet; an abundant supply of rope, cord, and string of several thicknesses; packing-needles, gun and ammunition, and fishing-rod.

Instruments:—Watch, two azimuth compasses, binocular telescope, parallel ruler, Olsen's Map of Iceland, and aneroid barometer.

Medicine:—Some mild aperient, laudanum, carbolic acid, glycerine; a good liniment, in case of sprains, should also be taken, such as the following—Opodeldoc, tincture of arnica, spirits of hartshorn, and camphor liniment, one part of each; two or three surgical bandages, and some cotton wool, in case of accident.

The cost of the trip:—Passage from Edinburgh to Iceland, including wine and fees, can never be really put down under 10*l*. each way, which is the sum it cost me upon each occasion.

As horses are the only means of transport in the island, one horse at least is needed for each man, and for every seventy pounds of luggage. If speed is an object, two horses for each man, and two for every seventy pounds of luggage are required. It is, however, a very good plan to start from Reykjavick with a single horse for each load, and buy fresh ones as you proceed. Two pack boxes are required for each horse; they cost from five to seven dollars a pair, good pack saddles five to seven dollars each, riding saddles thirty to fifty dollars, and bridles about five to nine dollars; the two latter may be taken from England with advantage. The cost of pack horses is from fifty to sixty rix-dollars, and that of a good riding horse seventy to a hundred dollars. The charge for a guide is two dollars and-a-half per day, with board, and one horse found him; and when travelling upon the Jökulls, three dollars per man. When stopping at a farm, the proper charge is eight skillings for each horse, half-a-dollar for each man, if he finds his own provisions, and one dollar when he does not. When a tent is pitched, and the whole party remain in it, the horses should be paid for at the above rate. Everything supplied from the farm should be paid for, at a previously arranged price, and one dollar given to the farmer as gratuity. The dates at which the steamer leaves Scotland for Iceland can be obtained at any post office, and the cost of an expedition can be fairly reckoned by the above scale of expenses. All cases of extortion should be rigorously objected to, and when more than a fair price is demanded it should on no account be given, and the proper recompense alone be tendered. A strict adherence to these rules will save the traveller infinite annoyance and expense, and will render travelling more easy for future tourists.

The prices of everything may, of course, undergo some change, but if the Icelanders are wise they will not increase them beyond those I have quoted.

I would not advise anyone to go to Iceland who could not spare a clear month in the island. There is some delay consequent to the purchase of horses, hiring of guides, &c., and when they are in immediate requisition there is an increase in the price demanded. But delay can be avoided by sending out money, and ordering all required by the steamer previous to that by which the traveller starts; but, as may be supposed, it is an expensive way of going to work. At the end of the trip everything that remains can generally be sold for about one-sixth of the original cost.

The Icelanders generally are short and sturdy, very honest and trustworthy, and very reticent; I never met but two who could appreciate any kind of joke. Their work in summer consists in fishing, tending sheep and cattle, gathering hay, digging turf, and collecting fuel. In winter, tending their stock, spinning and preparing their homespun cloth (wadmal); they show some skill in the rougher kinds of jewellery, also in carpentering and smith's work, especially the latter. Their dress (particularly that of the men) is rapidly becoming like our own, with the exception of skin shoes, resembling the North-American Indian mocassin, but without tops, and their cloth is generally the homespun wadmal, which is very warm and strong. The usual dress of the women is a bodice, over which is worn a tight jacket (often knitted) and a petticoat of homespun cloth; on their heads they wear a small round cap with long silk tassel hanging on one side. Upon grand occasions they wear a gayer costume, often enriched with gold and silver braiding, and a tall white helmet-like cap, called a "faldr," from which depends a veil. I have rarely seen this costume, and I believe the European style of dress is greatly taking its place.

The old houses are built of lava blocks thatched with turf, upon which a good crop of grass often grows; they are "chinked" with moss and turf, and generally lack means of ventilation. The more recent erections, whether of house or church, are built of wooden framework, and are a decided improvement upon the old style, though I should think they must be rather cold in winter. The principal food is fish, mutton, butter, milk, coffee, rye-bread cakes, and corn brandy (schnapps), although, of course, many European articles of diet and luxury are rapidly being introduced. The universal article of diet is the stock-fish. It is the ling, split open and dried; this is never cooked, but it is bruised and pounded upon a large stone which every Icelander keeps outside his house door for that purpose; the flesh is then stripped off in filaments, and eaten with butter or grease. These filaments are perfectly tasteless, and are not unlike asbestos in appearance, though I must say they are in a degree nutritious. As a rule, the Icelanders do not suffer from want of food, though their peculiar *penchant* for raw dried meat and fish, and sometimes putrid food, cannot be very conducive to health, and it is decidedly favourable to scorbutic diseases; but potatoes and turnips, which are grown for a short time at the end of summer, supply them with some vegetable food. The taste for raw and putrid food is happily decreasing. As a nation, the people are well educated, though it is scarcely true to say that erudition and abstract learning are national characteristics. They all have a plain and simple education, and have a great love for poetry and literature, for which they were much celebrated four or five centuries ago. Printing was introduced into the island between the years 1527 and 1530, A.D., by a Swede, named John Mathieson, and the first work, *Breviarium Nidarosiense*, was printed at Hoolar, in the north of the island.

The physical characteristics of the Icelandic scenery are grandeur and desolation. Except Reykjavick, I have seen neither towns, nor villages, nor roads—nothing but single farms, many of which have about them several habitations belonging to the owner, his tenants and servants. The highways are mere bridle-tracks, worn by the hoofs of ponies. Fruit trees there are none, and the only berries are the blauberry and craigberry. There is now no timber, though from some of the ancient sagas and the trunks of trees, &c., dug up in many of the marshes, it would appear that timber formerly grew in Iceland; at present nothing grows but low scrub, and that by no means abundantly. The climate appears to have undergone a great change, perhaps in consequence of the increase of the large ice Jökulls and some alteration in the disposition and annual flow of the Greenland floating ice; the former cause, perhaps, is consequent on the latter. The winter commences in the middle of October and ends in April; the climate is greatly tempered by the Gulf stream which washes the south shore.

Iceland was settled in the ninth century by refugees from Norway; they found inhabitants there who were Christians and whom they designated Papas, which is conjectured to mean priests. This is confirmed by the preface of the "Land nama Book," or Book of Colonization, written by various authors, the earliest of whom is Ari the learned, born in 1068, and he expressly says, in the first chapter of the book, that Iceland was settled by the Norwegians in the time of King Alfred of England and Edward his son. He also mentions that Beda speaks of Iceland under the name of Thyle, more than a hundred years before the arrival of the Norwegians, and that they found there Irish books, bells, and crosiers, which prove that these people came from the west; and it is added that the English books mention an intercourse at those times. King Alfred certainly mentions in his translation of "Orosius" the utmost land to the NW. of Iceland, called Thila, and that is known to few on account of its great distance. See Alfred's "Orosius," page 31. The "Land nama Book" was published at Copenhagen in 1774. The circumstance of Irish books being left in Iceland is likewise mentioned by the same Ari, in "Ara Multiscii Shedis dé Icelandia," Oxoniæ, 1716, chap. ii., page 10— "They chose not to live with the heathens, and for that reason went away, leaving behind Irish books, bells, and crosiers." It is clear that Iceland was populated long before we first hear of the Norwegians visiting it, and there is every reason to suppose that the inhabitants enjoyed a much better climate than at the present time. The first Norwegian who reached Iceland was a Viking, named Naddoddr, in 861, who was compelled, owing to stress of weather, to seek shelter in one of its Fjords. He named it Snioland (Snowland). He returned to Norway with such a glowing description of the country that he induced several adventurers to visit it, and among them an explorer of the name of Folke, who brought back a a very different and an unfavourable report. The Norwegian settlers were Ingolfr and Leifr, who after making a voyage to the country in 874, resolved to settle there. Emigration to Iceland now began to increase, in spite of great opposition from the King of Norway, who at length imposed a fine of four ounces of fine silver upon all emigrants. Soon an unsettled state of things began. Petty feuds disturbed the population, until, in 928, a leader was chosen, with the title of "Laug Saugumadur." He was elected by the assembled chiefs, and acted as arbitrator and speaker at public assemblies. He also proclaimed the laws, which were determined upon by the assembled chiefs. This was the commencement of the Althing; but intestine troubles and strifes so demoralized the country, that the Icelanders in 1261 put themselves under the protection of Hakan, King of Norway, and eventually with Norway became subject to Denmark. They were governed by an admiral, who was sent thither every year to make the necessary regulations; but afterwards a governor was appointed who resided permanently in the country: this form of government continued till the present year.

The Courts of Iceland are the Herads-thing or County Court, and the Superior Court, or Althing, from which, until the present year, an appeal lay to the Supreme Court of Denmark.

The early Christian religion was soon stamped out of the island, and Paganism became general, and there is no record of the reintroduction of

Christianity into the country until Bishop Frederic arrived from Saxony, in 981. After some opposition the country was Christianized, and in the twelfth century monks and convents abounded, and Iceland zealously contributed both men and money to the Crusades. King Christian III. of Norway introduced the Lutheran form of religion in 1540; but, owing to the great opposition of the Roman Catholic Bishops and Clergy, he did not succeed in establishing it until 1551, since which time the Icelandic Church has reposed in rest and tranquillity.

Many relics of the ancient Roman Church still exist throughout the island. There are eighty-nine parishes in Iceland, the pastors of which receive a small salary in addition to the contributions received from their congregations.

Although Iceland is a healthy country, the people are, as a whole, by no means long-lived: it is a rare thing to meet with men of seventy years of age; but I believe the women attain to a greater longevity than the men. These islanders suffer a great deal from skin diseases and rheumatic affections; but the most remarkable maladies are leprosy and the tapeworm, or the embryo form, "echino-coccus." The Icelandic leprosy differs entirely from "lepra arabum." The former commences with lowness of spirits, swelling of the extremities, and sometimes of other parts of the body. The skin becomes shiny and of a bluish cast, the hair falls off, the senses fail, boils break out, which develope into wounds, and terminate in death. This disease and the "lepra elephantiasis" is supposed to have been produced in the first instance by poorness and badness of living, and exposure in the first stages. It is not infectious, and can generally be cured. However, it has been happily on the decline ever since vegetable diet has become more general, and the people have lived better; and it is to be hoped now the taste for bad and putrid food is dying out, that this terrible disorder will die out with it.

Iceland is singularly destitute of ruins or architectural remains, the principal objects of historical interest being particular localities which have been immortalized by some tragical occurrence, the circumstances of which have been commemorated by the ancient poetical literature, such as the Logsberg at Thingvellir. "There are the remains of only two castles throughout the island; one near Videdal and the other near the parsonage of Skaggestad at Laugernas. At Midfiord, Godale and Vidvik, there are likewise the remains of what are supposed to be heathen temples." All other monuments of the ancient history of Iceland are but rude cairns and blocks of stone, which commemorate particular events or customs, such as the block of stone in plate No. 3, opposite the church at Thingvellir, whereon the ancient Icelanders regulated their measurements; or the cairns of Herdis and Kris, between Herdisuvick and Krisuvick.

The principal monuments of Iceland are literary ones. In the first place, the Icelanders have preserved to us the mythology of the Scandinavian nations, under the form of the books popularly known as the older and the younger Eddas, the poetic or the prose.

The older Edda is a collection of such poetic fragments of the ancient mythology of Scandinavia as was still current in Iceland in the twelfth century. The younger Edda is a prose and later work which traditionally bears the name of Gurdi, the historical. It is a compilation which amplifies and, in some places, fills up gaps in the earlier Edda.

There is also the form of composition known as Sagas by the Icelanders, which are mostly legendary histories of affairs which took place in Norway and Iceland from the ninth to the thirteenth centuries. It should be mentioned that there is mingled with the prose of these works a great deal of verse, exceedingly intricate in its character and metaphorical in diction, to the extent of often proving a puzzle for learned Icelanders themselves. Besides the above-named, there are many other poems chiefly of a religious character, which are of a later date, as, for example, "The Lily." The Icelandic literature of the last century is by no means inconsiderable, a great deal of which is of a devotional character. There is likewise a good translation of the "Odyssey" and of "Paradise Lost."

The most ancient literature of this country is no exception to that of others. It is universally poetical; nor does this feature in ancient history appear at all surprising, when we consider that at the time of composition the knowledge of letters was by no means general, and consequently the way of perpetuating the knowledge of such poems was to learn them by heart, and to repeat them at all gatherings or on public occasions, and in order to do so the rhythmical measure must have been of infinite assistance to the memory.

The principal rocks I have met with in this island are either igneous in their origin or derivatives from igneous rocks; they are basalts, tufas, agglomerates, and erupted lavas.

NOTES.

1, page 15. "Twæ Bakka" is a little Danish *biscuit*, generally eaten with coffee, meaning the two-backed, and is similar to our own biscuit commonly called "tops and bottoms."

2, p. 23. "Hafnarfjordite" is a basaltic rock, consisting of lime-oligoclase-feldspar and augite. It is only found at Hafnfjord, a small bay upon the south of Iceland, from which place it takes its name.

3, p. 33. "Agglomerate." I have used this word universally, instead of the words palagonite tufa, which has been generally used by Icelandic travellers, and I think it is more descriptive of the heterogenous character of the rock. I fear, however, the word conglomerate has in one or two places in this book accidentally crept in; the reader will, therefore, be kind enough, except where I speak of the deposits of the springs at Laugerdarlr, to read agglomerate for conglomerate wherever it may occur. The rock in question is really a palagonitic agglomerate. It is composed of disintegrated volcanic rocks and pulverent volcanic products, which cement together huge quantities of fragments of rock, cinders, &c. This agglomerate occurs universally in almost all the parts of Iceland that I have visited. It is formed in two ways—either suddenly during volcanic eruptions (as described on page 77), or by the gentle action of the streams and atmospheric elements, which collect together around the base of the mountains, during the lapse of long periods, precisely the same constituents which form the agglomerate of more terrible manufacture, and by long continuation of their gentler forces produce a similar, and perhaps more durable result.

4, p. 69. I have since learned that this worm is entirely innocuous when the food containing it is cooked.

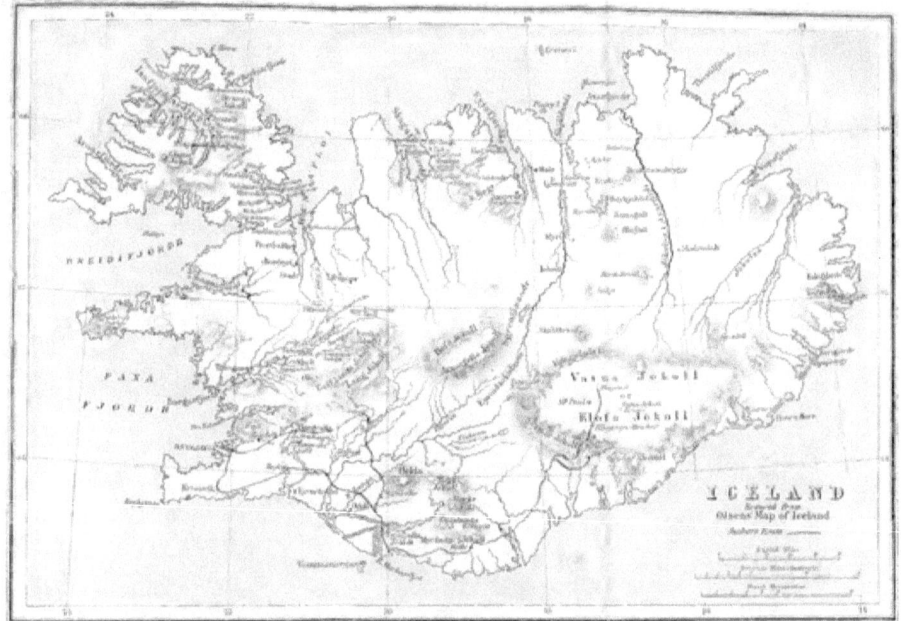

FLORA OF ICELAND.

The flora of Iceland is much more extensive than might be supposed from its latitude, owing to the excellent soil afforded by the disintegrated volcanic rocks and the salutary effect of the Gulf Stream, which washes the south shore of Iceland. Considering these two favourable circumstances, the absence of trees in Iceland and the pallor of the Icelandic flowers is somewhat remarkable. This, however, may be explained by the great absence of sunshine, the chilling influence of the huge and numerous ice Jökulls, and the nipping blasts of the N. and NW. wind from the Polar ice. The flora is essentially European, and there are only sixty-two species which are not natives of Great Britain.

www.ingramcontent.com/pod-product-compliance
Lightning Source LLC
Chambersburg PA
CBHW031818220426
43662CB00007B/707